Selected Poems

Also by Jon Silkin

The Psalms with their Spoils

Selected Poems

Jon Silkin

Routledge & Kegan Paul

LONDON, BOSTON AND HENLEY

This collection
first published in 1980
by Routledge & Kegan Paul Ltd
39 Store Street,
London WC1E 7DD,
9 Park Street, Boston,
Mass. 02108, USA and
Broadway House,
Newtown Road,
Henley-on-Thames,
Oxon RG9 1EN
Set in IBM Journal 11pt by Columns
and printed in Great Britain by
Lowe & Brydone Printers Ltd.
Thetford, Norfolk

British Library Cataloguing in Publication Data

Silkin, Jon

Selected poems.
821'.9'14   PR6037.15   80-40610

ISBN 0 7100 0614 4

Contents

Note

The question as to whether one changes one's work 'at a later date' is a troublesome one, but I would not hesitate to change that work if I thought I was improving it. The problem is to do with what one presently thinks, for what one thought is different from what one now thinks. The distinction I'm offering embodies the principle I've adopted. Certain poems I've written now seem beyond my inspection. I re-wrote parts of 'Furnished Lives', for instance, which was originally published in *The Two Freedoms* (1958); and I published the re-written poem in my earlier *Selected Poems* (1966). I could not think of re-writing that poem again, even supposing I wished to. But for this selection I have, to take a later poem, managed to re-think myself into 'Harebell' to the extent of omitting the first six lines of the original version. And with regard to the exclusion of parts of poems, I've cut the 'middle section' of the long poem 'Amana Grass' because I didn't any longer like the kind of argument the poem employed there, although I still like the poem itself.

As far as *The People* (*The Principle of Water*, 1976) is concerned, I had a different problem, and a more complex one. Originally, I was trying to fit narrative and image to each other, and I think that although the more narrative parts of the poem — the sections about Camps — worked, as far as I was concerned, the imagistic parts of the poem were more concerned with righting their corresponding balance and weight than was probably good for them. Moreover, there were also parts of the poem that hovered uneasily between, in this composite, and had not then settled into some new substance that would result from a fusing of both narrative and image. When I came to re-write what I thought, and still think, of as a poem within my present grasp — a poem I was still 'with' — I both cut out and re-wrote on the basis of the kind of argument I was having with myself, and to which I've just referred. So the result is not merely a shorter poem but, in some ways, a re-written one. I should like the present version of *The People* to be regarded as a new and *complete* version, not a selection from the parts of an earlier version.

I think of time as a dimension consisting, among other things, of one's relations with others. And as a poet, my relations are not merely with a reader but with those who published or criticized my work — my active readers. It is *my* pleasure (to quote Roy Fisher) to name names. I owe my first help and encouragement to Philip Inman; and to Dannie Abse, I owe his publishing me in his *Poetry and Poverty*. The late C. Day Lewis was responsible for my being published, for fifteen years, by Chatto & Windus. I am grateful for that, and to him for a great deal else besides. To the American poet, Gene Baro, years of careful reading; and I owe something like thirty years of critical reading to the novelist and poet Emanuel Litvinoff. I have benefited for nearly twenty years from the attentive reading of the poet and critic Jon Glover. George MacBeth was 'poetry editor' for the BBC for many years (as was also Terence Tiller), and MacBeth first broadcast the 'Flower Poems'. John Barrell first published many of them (in *Grantas*). John Scotney produced an earlier (and longer) version of *The People*, and the actors in that production were Miriam Margolyes, Nigel Anthony and John Rowe.

I record my years of friendship with three American readers, Ed Brunner, Steve Holmes and Robert Ober. But my first and longest friendship *in* America was with the critic Merle Brown, who died in December 1978. From 1965 I was in contact with Merle Brown, firstly at Denison University, Ohio, and then, until his death, at the University of Iowa. Our relations, as friends, and as critic and poet, were never uneventful, often disturbing. I have benefited from my contact with the poet Geoffrey Hill over a period of eight years at Leeds, and I am grateful for the reading of my work given me by Raymond Gardner. I have benefited from the reading given me by Catherine Lamb; and by the fellow-poet and fellow-editor, Ken Smith. Together we edited *Stand* (with Catherine Lamb) for six years. I must thank Tony Rudolf (then of *European Judaism* and now of his own Menard Press) and I wish to thank Martin Booth of the Sceptre Press. I am grateful to Michael Schmidt and his Carcanet New Press for the publishing of *The Principle of Water*, and for his involvement, with George Stephenson of MidNag, over *The Little Time-keeper*. And I am grateful to Michael Wilding for his publishing these last two with Wild and Woolley in Australia. Wesleyan University Press, W.W. Norton (from *The Little Time-keeper*, copyright © 1976 by Jon Silkin, reprinted by permission of W.W. Norton & Company), and Bruce Chandler of the Heron Press published my books in the US. I also wish to record, with especial reference to *The Little Time-keeper* poems, the careful attention given by the poet Rodney Pybus. The Index was compiled by David and Linda Wise.

Lastly, I thank my wife, the short-story writer Lorna Tracy, with whose balance, judgment and clear-eyed wit I note my deficiencies. That true statement does not take full account of her sympathetic reading of my work, nor of my impatience with myself. There are others I could acknowledge, and more of them more recently. But those latter, whom I should like to name, fall outside the time-span of the work printed here.

J.S.

from

The Peaceable Kingdom

Carved

Two small dogs stood by a dead black bird
And the black bird was very dead.

The two dogs stood by the bird like large lions
But they never touched the dead thing, once.

They would like to have eaten the black thing
But it was very dead with red ants

Sawing its neck away like stone masons
And the red ants were very much alive.

So all the time the dogs stood they barked there
Because they couldn't eat the black thing.

Something large about that black bird.
It was being eaten by red death

While the two large-lion small dogs just stood,
Barking: they never touched the black thing,

And the black thing never looked at them, once.
It was indifferent to two small dogs.

Maybe it did not hear those large lions
Or maybe the black bird felt sorry for the small dogs.

Meanwhile the dead went on being dead and the living
        living.

A Death to Us

A tiny fly fell down on my page
Shivered, lay down, and died on my page.

I threw his body onto the floor
That had laid its frail life next to mine.

His death then became an intrusion on
My action; he claimed himself as my victim.

His speck of body accused me there
Without an action, of his small brown death.

And I think now as I barely perceive him
That his purpose became in dying, a demand

For a murderer of his casual body.
So I must give his life a meaning

So I must carry his death about me
Like a large fly, like a large frail purpose.

A Space in the Air

The first day he had gone
I barely missed him. I was glad almost he had left
    Without a bark or flick of his tail,
        I was content he had slipped

    Out into the world. I felt,
Without remarking, it was nearly a relief
        From his dirty habits. Then, the second
        Day I noticed the space

    He left behind him. A hole
Cut out of the air. And I missed him suddenly,
        Missed him almost without knowing
            Why it was so. And I grew

    Afraid he was dead, expecting death
As something I had grown used to. I was afraid
        The clumsy children in the street
            Had cut his tail off as

    A souvenir of the living and
I did not know what to do. I grew afraid
        Somebody had hurt him. I called his name
            But the hole in the air remained.

    I have grown accustomed to death
Lately. But his absence made me sad,
        I do not know how he should do it
            But his absence frightened me.

It was not only his death I feared,
Not only his, but as if all of those
    I loved, as if all those near me
        Should suddenly go

    Into the hole in the light
And disappear. As if all of them should go
    Without barking, without speaking,
        Without noticing me there

    But go; and going as if
The instrument of pain were a casual thing
    To suffer, as if they should suffer so,
        Casually, and without greatness,

    Without purpose even. But just go.
I should be afraid to lose all those friends like this.
    I should fear to lose those loves. But mostly
        I should fear to lose you.

    If you should go
Without affliction, but even so, I should fear
    The rent you would make in the air
        And the bare howling

    Streaming after your naked hair.
I should feel your going down more than my going down.
    My own death I bear every day
        More or less

But your death would be something else,
Something else beyond me. It would not be
     Your death or my death, love,
        But our rose-linked dissolution.

    So I feared his going,
His death, not our death, but a hint at our death. And
          I shall always fear
     The death of those we love as
       The hint of your death, love.

Death of a Son

(who died in a mental hospital aged one)

Something has ceased to come along with me.
Something like a person: something very like one.
And there was no nobility in it
Or anything like that.

Something was there like a one year
Old house, dumb as stone. While the near buildings
Sang like birds and laughed
Understanding the pact

They were to have with silence. But he
Neither sang nor laughed. He did not bless silence
Like bread, with words.
He did not forsake silence.

But rather, like a house in mourning
Kept the eye turned in to watch the silence while
The other houses like birds
Sang around him.

And the breathing silence neither
Moved nor was still.

I have seen stones: I have seen brick
But this house was made up of neither bricks nor stone
But a house of flesh and blood
With flesh of stone

And bricks for blood. A house
Of stones and blood in breathing silence with the other
    Birds singing crazy on its chimneys.
      But this was silence,

  This was something else, this was
Hearing and speaking though he was a house drawn
    Into silence, this was
      Something religious in his silence,

  Something shining in his quiet,
This was different this was altogether something else:
    Though he never spoke, this
      Was something to do with death.

  And then slowly the eye stopped looking
Inward. The silence rose and became still.
The look turned to the outer place and stopped,
    With the birds still shrilling around him.
      And as if he could speak

He turned over on his side with his one year
Red as a wound
He turned over as if he could be sorry for this
And out of his eyes two great tears rolled, like stones, and
      he died.

First it was Singing

From the first cry
I was given music with which to speak,
Tramping the agape streets
The amazed faces

Turning, with their
Voices to laugh at the singer in the common
Street. From the first I was
Given a voice

To cry out with.
It was a peaceable music tuned in fear.
Later, it was death
But it was singing

First.
And from that it was I loved the hopping birds,
The limping fly
And the mad

Bee, stung to anger
In worship of summer. It was their speech, and my speech,
The Jewish stone and the
Animal rock

Rolling together that made me sing
Of our common lash, the white raised weal across
Our black back, I and
The hunted fox, the

Huge fly, his
Dangerous wings torn from his body
The seal tusking the sea,
As the dog bawls air.

It was our harm
Made me sing. Afterwards it was death,
Death of the stone
By stoning

The animal
By animals, but, first, singing.
Jew and animal singing first;
And afterwards, death.

Caring for Animals

I ask sometimes why these small animals
With bitter eyes, why we should care for them.

I question the sky, the serene blue water,
But it cannot say. It gives no answer.

And no answer releases in my head
A procession of grey shades patched and whimpering;

Dogs with clipped ears, wheezing cart horses,
A fly without shadow and without thought.

Is it with these menaces to our vision
With this procession led by a man carrying wood

We must be concerned? The holy land, the rearing
Green island should be kindlier than this.

Yet the animals, our ghosts, need tending to.
Take in the whipped cat and the blinded owl;

Take up the man-trapped squirrel upon your shoulder.
Attend to the unnecessary beasts.

From growing mercy and a moderate love
Great love for the human animal occurs.

And your love grows. Your great love grows and grows.

Hunger

A woman goes to feed her friends each day.
She moves slowly, she stoops, and in her hand

Is the offering of bread which she hurls with all her love
At the large sparrows, she attacks them with it. But they

Only leap at her as she strides outside her house.
For they know by her carriage and her stooping pride

She is of them. She is full of hunger for
The hand that bears the profound gift of love.

But like them she is inarticulate
She nods and pecks when she would give her heart.

Her body stoops but the straight spirit burns
And while she is dying the black sky watches her.

For David Emanuel

I shall pass you the tall moment.
It was on the still day I saw my son
Lying in his sleep. The birds,
Clamoring, they

Poked their shining faces
In the child's window. That was a shy day,
The sun walking through the mist,
The pale hours

Following his first
Day when we ran in through the solid, brass
Light, alive to this life.
And this day, I stole

Into the small sleeping
Room of his dreaming and saw him, half
Of my sure flesh, strong
To be surer yet

Of his unabiding flesh.
It wasn't the ripe glory of the sun
Nor the dogs grinning below
At a mouldy joy bone.

It was my son. Half Jew
And wholly human sleeping in the curved eye
Of his future. And I
Alone with the sun in

Its morning, I with
Two large eyes staring into his god's eyes:
He was half mine, half
That woman buried

In the hot raiments of her sleep.
I could not wholly wake him. But I turned to the
Intruding sun that
Stole so

Fearfully in his room. I
Thanked it that this morning it touched my eyes that
They flung wide to
The joy of my son,

That he entered and shook my love,
And took my heart into his small heart. May love like this
Remain with him, as the innocence
Of the sky remains crowned with the sun.

from _____
The Two
Freedoms

The Two Freedoms

There were two birds today
Broke from their cage and seemed as gold until
 In the dry sun, their bodies were
Transfigured; they hung like ghosts possessed with the
             silence
 But not with the shapelessness of
Spirits; they, in the sun flashed one gold flown

 Through another;
And then were quiet on the broad, trunked back
 Of the wood chair. They were
Inviolable, with that power and helplessness
 Which sculpture has. The sunlight
Smoked on them, gold were their wings, gold feet; gold
   sounds

 Fled from their throats quickened by
The winged sun that, for a moment, urged their flesh
 To the transubstantial freedom
Ghosts are. They in the sun became the one gold
 With him in dignity.
I caught and put them back into their cage.

 Surely, I thought, Man is
ridiculous whose avarice for life
 Is that he must put life
Back in a cage, cage life; he will increase
 The flow of the cruel gland,
Then watch, then feel his power and its rage

Grow and be satisfied.
I shut the cage door, I looked with a cold rage
At their stretched screams of pain,
And I thought again of the stairs down which the world
Turns from its prison to
The cage of the still prison; turns and is caged.

And thought, but it is best
That they fly in their cage and do not learn
Of that grey, ironic flight
From one space to another, but step down
From their carriage in the air
To that humble, iron house. Safely the breast

Has shed that gold
Which had perched, for an instant, on their flesh.
But as these careful words
Turned in my mind, their cry like a stab pierced
Me; I thought of my own
Wings, cut and trimmed by my grey God.

Furnished Lives

I have been walking today
Where the sour children of London's poor sleep
Pressed close to the unfrosted glare.
Torment lying closed in tenement,
Of the clay fire; I
Have watched their whispering souls fly straight to God:

'O Lord, please give to us
A dinner-service, austere, yet gay: like snow
When swans are on it; Bird,
Unfold your wings until like a white smile
You fill this mid-white room.'
I have balanced myself on the meagre Strand where

Each man and woman turn,
On the deliberate hour of the cock
As if two new risen souls,
Through the cragged landscape in each other's eyes.
But where lover upon lover
Should meet — where sheet, and pillow, and eiderdown

Should frolic, and crisp,
As dolphins on the stylized crown of the sea
Their pale cerements lie.
They tread with chocolate souls and paper hands;
They walk into that room
Your gay and daffodil smile has never seen;

Not to love's pleasant feast
They go, in the mutations of the night,
        But to their humiliations
Paled as a swan's dead feather scorched in the sun.
        I have been walking today
Among the newly paper-crowned, among those

        Whose casual, paper body
Is crushed between fate's fingers and the platter;
        But Sir, their perpetual fire
Was not stubbed out, folded on brass or stone
        Extinguished in the dark,
But burns with the drear dampness of cut flowers.

        I cannot hear their piped
Cry. These souls have no players. They have resigned
        The vivid performance of their world.
                And your world, Lord,
                    Has now become
Like a dumb winter show, held in one room,

        Which must now reek of age
Before you have retouched its lips with such straight fire
        As through your stony earth
Burns with ferocious tears in the world's eyes:
Church-stone, door-knocker, and polished railway lines
        Move in their separate dumb way
                So why not these lives:
I ask you often, but you never say?

Death of a Bird

After those first days
When we had placed him in his iron cage
   And made a space for him
      From such

Outrageous cage of wire,
Long and shallow, where the sunlight fell
   Through the air, onto him;
      After

He had been fed for three days
Suddenly, in that sunlight before noon
   He was dead with no
      Pretence.

He did not say goodbye
He did not say thankyou, but he died then
   Lying flat on the rigid
      Wires

Of his cage, his gold
Beak shut tight, which once in hunger had
   Opened as a trap
      And then

Swiftly closed again,
Swallowing quickly what I had given him;
   How can I say I am sorry
      He died.

Seeing him lie there dead,
Death's friend with death, I was angry he
Had gone without pretext or warning,
With no

Suggestion first he should go,
Since I had fed him, then put wires round him
Bade him hop across
The bars of my hands.

I asked him only that
He should desire his life. He had become
Of us a black friend with
A gold mouth

Shrilly singing through
The heat. The labour of the black bird! I
Cannot understand why
He is dead.

I bury him familiarly.
His heritage is a small brown garden.
Something is added to the everlasting earth;
From my mind a space is taken away.

Bowl

The beggar's bowl is formed from hands.
Hunger keeps them there, rigid; inside
Crouches a blessing from the sun;
Below; the dried bones of starvation.

No milk; and no wine.
You, into this gnarled hand put
Bread, and drop meat; raw,
Boned and moist, but donate no pity.

And I turned from the Inner Heart

And I turned from the inner heart having no further cause
To look there, to pursue what lay inside,
And moved to the world not as I would have world
But as it lay before me, as a map lies open
Unalterable through what it signifies, without vision
Or fantasy, yet full with promise. And although

The world as I had known it I replenished
Only with the dreams of the man who lies in sickness
Although I believed in that reconstruction of hope
I knew a world, as replete with misery
As the bowl the beggar raises, empty, yet full
With the dried bones of starvation, as the cup denied

Milk, death before milk; and I turned to the outer
Place, although as I knew I could not hope
To care for those who were there, netiher for what they
            might be
Nor for what they were, meanness scrubbed into the face,
The naked bone of the face in sleep
Not tender now nor cruel but as the stone,

Instrument to be used, to be kept sharp for
The brass fiction of the industrial King
Who is inviolate; but who is yet intact
From Human Agony. So that I cried, Lord,
I am not surprised with your Word, but regard now
Your tin world. Is *this* your vision? Straightway the whirr

Of the indefatigable machine filled the wheel-dark air.
And the worker cried, 'This is the terrible, real world
Of the beggar's bowl, which lies empty, world whose image is
Refracted by a brass screw. Our dreams are wound
Within the coil of tungsten. The beggar's bowls are broken;
But our world lies open like a map of hope!'

from _____
The
Re-ordering
of the Stones

The Area of Conflict

Searching how to relieve
The piled cacophony of
My spiritual unrest, I
Mistward that morning went.
Everywhere on glass it
Had globuled moist hands.
And though behind doors sleep
Hung webbed, larksvoice with
Spit glittered on the glass
Loosening fear's cloy.
I moved like a doomed leaf
Taking a path alight
With dew, which crept into
A field, burning with flesh.
I said to one who raked
Up arms and teeth and hair
And human bone and hair
Into that fire again
'What are you making here?'
Though he did not reply
Turning apart between
The cold heats. I asked, 'do you see
This flesh still lives, clinging
To its life, and is loth
To slide from its lapbone?'
He raised up to his mouth
The sneering lip we dread
Closing his fingers on
A complete silence. Sky dropped
Down tears in blood, I think.

The Measure

We all cry for love;
But what if we get it? To hold
In sex, and affection,
The adored human creature
Making of both a unit
In love, and procreate
Which is the end of love,
Drops one small image into
A widening universe.
Man's love disintegrates
In the spaces void of him;
And gradually he comes
To know that he is small.
What is man's love? To hold
Into despair the loved creature,
And propagate an image
Is the utmost. Beyond his tides
The chronic invalids
Of broken universes
Wait in derision on man.
Yet he was formed to love.
Earth cries, sun cries,
With the stark, hapless Gods
Phenomenal of matter
In space, to this end.
But when man reaches this
And grows into himself,
He dwindles to his size.
His spaces melt into him

He occupies no area.
Love then is the space of destruction,
And but for the harmonies
Of despair, he is nothing.
Weep, then, to be a stone
Or a cold animal
In servitude to something
Other than consciousness
Which love brings; since that shape
Or measure, in awareness
Through love of what we are,
Is that measure of space death is.

Astringencies

1 *The Coldness*

Where the printing-works buttress a church
And the northern river like moss
Robes herself slowly through
The cold township of York,
More slowly than usual
For a cold northern river,
You see the citizens
Indulging stately pleasures,
Like swans. But they seem cold.
Why have they been so punished;
In what do their sins consist now?
An assertion persistent
As a gross tumour, and the sense
Of such growth haunting
The flesh of York
Is that there has been
No synagogue since eleven ninety
When eight hundred Jews
Took each other's lives
To escape christian death
By christian hand; and the last
Took his own. The event
Has the frigid persistence of a growth
In the flesh. It is a fact
No other fact can be added to
Save that it was Easter, the time
When the dead christian God

Rose again. It is in this,
Perhaps, they are haunted; for the cold
Blood of victims is colder,
More staining, more corrosive
On the soul, than the blood of martyrs.
What consciousness is there of the cold
Heart, with its spaces?
For nothing penetrates
More than admitted absence.
The heart in warmth, even, cannot
Close its gaps. Absence of Jews
Through hatred, or indifference,
A gap they slip through, a conscience
That corrodes more deeply since it is
Forgotten — this deadens York.
Where are the stone-masons, the builders
Skilled in glass, strong first in wood;
Taut, flaxen plumbers with lengths of pipe,
Steel rules coiled in their palms;
The printers; canopy-makers —
Makers in the institution of marriage?
Their absence is endless, a socket
Where the jaw is protected neither
Through its tolerance for tooth,
Nor for blood. Either there is pain or no pain.
If they could feel; were there one
Among them with this kind
Of sensitivity that
Could touch the dignity,
Masonry of the cold
Northern face that falls
As you touch it, there might

Be some moving to
A northern expurgation.
All Europe is touched
With some of frigid York,
As York is now by Europe.

2 *Asleep?*

Today, I want to speak
Of human agony.
It makes most men
Very sure that pain
Can be eliminated.
If pain were suffering
This were so. But such agony
Is not a passion, but persists
A bruise in the being,
Because human tenderness
Is insufficient, or love
Which is not always tender,
Even refutes this passion.
What shall we do for pain,
Man's agony? If we wound
Only to kill, we are mad.
Deny love, and we inhume
The hunger we live by.
Yet without tenderness
We die. So we must live
Complexly, as befits
The bedraggled human condition
And being vigilant

Experience much of man
In the fibres, in these moral fibres.
For man's life in its pain
Is something like a jungle
Where everything that is
Is agony, in this sense:
That things war to survive.
Pain is complex, something akin
To a stone with veins of colour
In it, that cross and cross
But never reconcile
Into one swab of colour
Or the stone that contains them.

Respectabilities

Many liberals don't just
Make love, they first ask each other;
And either is free to decline
What the other wishes;
That is, unmitigated
Possession of the beloved's flesh.
Nothing hasty, nothing unconsidered
Catches the liberal by
The hairs of lust. Nothing.
And this consideration
For those feelings
Of the approached one naked
In love or in hunger
Is extended to all.
He will, for instance, ask
A starving man if he
Would eat, pressing
For the particulars
Of hunger. And enquire
Why he is deficient
In bread. All men are treated
With such perception as stones
Get in subjection to
Their shaper, as their use fits
To his. Men are chosen to meet
That judged compassion which
A liberal has. A wounded man
Receives the ointments of love
From matrons, with respect.

Sex, the inhuman hunger,
Demands courteous
Submission, polite domination.
In fact, the turning world
A stone delicately
Veined with acceptable
Colours, deficient just because
Another stone has gouged
A bit from its flesh
Demands the liberal heart;
Though a different stone
Brutal in the untamed
Components — a misshapen
Tongue of useless rock —
Merits, and gets,
A frank dismissal.
And this, too, is fair;
Though more than half the earth
Is denied purchase on
That delicate conscience
Cash gives: a fair if privileged
Mind veined with gold.

The Centre

My ancestors made love
In the hot pastures of the near east
And got me my seed there.
I should be drawn to
The Mediterranean.
I suppose I am. Greece
Was the shudder of the bird from the high hills.
But Italy; those with gold teeth
Are plucked of these by the Italian;
His main industry is fools.
His landscape gathers on the surface,
Not deepening into
The scents of heat, that delicate
Strength which breaks through
The white, Greek rock
In veins of darkness
That smell of the mineral
Origins of men.
So there is Greece. But my mind stays
In a place I saw little of.
The river drifts through
The town, falling massively
Under a low bridge.
Geneva. Was it fixed
I should choose your cool streets
Hinted of by the south?
Round this place move
The ornate schisms, intertwined
And made fast by the vicious and costly

Emblem of puissant Europe.
Is it strong only? It is also
Absurd. It is a continent
Caught in its intellect
At which centre it drops
Into a great lake;
Like some bath with its plug out.
And it is here I am
Constrained by having both
Prevailing intensities
As locked, and as formed
As the coolness is formed here
In precision from the clash
Of oppositions. Such firmness
Seems pre-determined
And intertwined to a gap
That is the weave and the space
Made by Europe in struggle,
Where choice flickers, but does not choose.
It is where the tensions meet
And wear each other away.
The life of a great
Intelligent continent
Falls through the space
It has made in itself
With too much intellect.
Or was it the intellect
Sought for a bride
But found only itself
Sufficient for its appetites, —
Say a poison this chemist
Fatally delivered
And tasted, and decayed on.

Warrior

Some division divided on itself
The parent world, in imperfect fruition,
Conceived as child in her children. All men
With all women, split between their single love
And their multifold, were born in thought,
But before them, thought as division was born.
World fits like a brain. God, making himself,
Since being made makes the flaw, is divided
On himself. As if air were a discord
We breathe division. What is division?
Man lies on rock, in a barren splendour,
Disaffected from himself, from rock,
Even division. Despair shall come,
And will tear him.

The Wall

Living as though a wall
Had been raised between each
of us, by compulsion, we share
These stones. At which some men
Would call this a failure
In communication. The fact is
Not Babel, but mutual despair
Separates us, since each
Through love, detachment, or exhaustion
Is himself alone, though each one,
By nature, lacks what the other has.
The walls remain. They are
A possession no man surrenders
But he perishes. And in his loneness
He beats on the barriers.
It is the agony
Which seems supreme, as stone
Triumphs in what it is
Though its manipulators
Give it whatever form
The conscious use demands,
For man is agony.

Depths

Textures. Why always textures?
The fuss. It is enough
You take and hold the thing:
That being warm it gives you
A special sense of permanence.
Since but for the whole shape
There would be no texture. Despair
Has texture. It is constructed
From a total helplessness.
Despair is texture; without it
We should not know how to face
The thing with such certainty
Of loss. But touching it
We very gently feel
The whole paralysis
Of agony give way
Into the steadfastnesses
Of reality,
The differing planes of surface
We cannot avoid contact with
Which employs the sunk depths.

Savings

I see the government
Is suggesting that some
Of us save money. A woman
Sitting at table with
A pen on her lips,
By her side the snap
Of her fiancé, writes
A letter: 'if we both save
We may have what we want
In a few years.' The order
For torturing wires and straps
A man and wife may use
Is already placed.
Meanwhile parliament debases
Such foul coinage
As these two save
On massive armaments.

I want a small clock;
I want a bed, a wardrobe
To hang my trousers in;
Also a kitchen in
Repair, for I want food.

But let me stay my soul
A little clean of her,
With something of the compassion
A strong woman has
Decently gentle. Death infinitely

Comes close when we are old:
Death of the soul is like
A pan of boiling milk,
The heat thieves it away
And something of the man
That might live after death
Precedes his flesh into
The soil in particles
Not smaller than dejection.
We are born part of the way
Death goes; but I pray the angelic forms
Help me to stay that bit
Until I die.

Sacred

I have talked with respectable women
Many of whom declare
The several fingered dew
Laid on a man's parts is love.
More naked is love; some say
Pure, like a glacier:
Yet congruous as despair,
Or rather something
Meaner than vanity.
For one with coarse-grained hand
Ties her sharp ribbon to
Her hair while, binding him,
Yells, 'love O love,' though she
Takes with an ancient care
Ever to give what is
Part of security.

There are others too, numerous
As sand-grain who sweat for
Not ambition but bread,
Having all but the seminal part
Of coarse men and cold men
Unenamoured of love
And love's perplexities.

So here, besides the cash
I give you a steel necklace
To be worn near the flesh
As conduit, a flow of

Hand-made steel ornamentation:
So many lesser than you
So many professing love
Less capable of that
And who are bought, and know it
May not pretend to passion.
Incapable of passion
They move with a rigid glare
Beneath their horror.

Nothing of tenderness
Will ever touch in them
For child or animal
Much generosity.

You to whom too much
Is given, but no love —
It is so much you give me
The tenderness you give now
Though that is bought from you,
That having little to offer
This much of you is more
Than others surrendering;
More than respectable women
More than such practised thieves.

**For a Child, on his being pronounced Mentally
Defective by a Committee of the LCC**

You are not like them.
Men learnèd with women, with rigid souls are pleased
To measure what gaps your brain has.

In those unstopped spaces your laughter howls
At their pure probing of your defective mind.
You shrink from

That heart defective of pity;
And you shrink from intelligence that with
Use of brutal wood bricks

Is decided, whatever
Lacuna impedes the delirious message of reason
You are subject to the wardress's care.

You are to throb in a house, where God's spat blood
With coughed bone, though mewed up in man's frame
Is not sinewed to intellect

But to memory of each flawed
Soul — confronts your passage out, building a cage
With bare bars of the iron

Some caged brains spattered
And the blood cursed
As it cooled on the metal.

The chill mind sits in the perfected
House, carefully pronouncing madness.

Yet how may the cold heart be sane;
How shall the naive intelligence be sane?
Since the pure mind that would love you has
Become discorporate of its love.

For the rooms they examined you in were loveless;
And the faces shaped like the pitiless wood
Were cold, inquiring, with that madness
Which understands not the purpose but
The applying of what it learned to do.

The chill man once more approaches your searched house.
Only may he perceive how to unlock the door
That conceals what you and he crave. The way
Through mind is a passage through doors love opens.
Love, only. If without love, he but glides
Through the cool strictures of his immoral intelligence.

But there are no locks to your house, child. The blown
Straws of man pass through you. You are howled
                              through by the elements.
Your love, and your fear which is fear of what is not love
Are detained by you:
But the heat and dispassion of the world press through you.

For though lit with love, your soul
That is not intelligenced yet
By reason, a darkness we increase,
Detains nothing.

Without darkness you strain nothing to you.

Perhaps the intelligences must darken
What permits the uncontrollable
Radiance passage. But love which
You have, remains
Undiminished through what madness ever light is.

Dedications

1 *To Tamasin, aged six*

White as a new-made cake
Tamasin, with long hair
Darkly hung slack,
It is little you ask for
Or any can ask: to speak
A few words, and be answered.
To solitary men
From isolated women,
But this much: with child's hand
As you, to hold in the clasps
The scant human affection
Rare as bread in the starving
If sun-clasped coasts of Africa
And hold it tight, a moment,
And never let it slip out,
In the clasp, like a hungry eye.
For the eye is the soul's eye
And this food that we give
We eat, whiter than you
Or children yet spotless
Having as purity
Their simple hunger.

2 *To my Friends*

It does not matter she never knew
Who Pater was. What is rare
Despite the encirclements of marriage
Or even the political relationships
Affianced beyond parliament
Is love, which breaks the breads.
The staff of women, the dread,
The hunger of men, it is not
Just what I am capable of
If mature; it is the force
Behind those intimations of our senses
Progenitor to more growth,
If anything is. Remember,
The moulds of rock perish,
The flower so delicately formed
The minute exactness seems meant
To last. What does live
In the complex fabrics of air,
Uncoloured, and always nubile,
Is this man-like attribute.
So very carefully
Consider what you do
As an action related always
To this eternal motion
In man's leathery breast;
For the way we treat each other
In private is, minutely,
The way we deal with wives
And they their men. Even stones
Wrinkled in a contempt

Of their manipulators
Lie in some comradeship,
For their sakes. And for Man,
Men matter, whether that God
Who made us, and the stones,
Is watching us, or bored
With human agony
Lies in immortal sleep
Terribly locked, not witnessing
The outrages of human hunger
Bearable only because
They must be, even these uptorn
Grains of love that are burned
In complex and primitive agonies
In concentration camps.

The Possibility

I accept all
Of what seems large,
The ship in the sea's unlovely
    Pressures. We cut

By as much
As we are pressed. Water
Begins its unsmiling hurts.
    Behind, the bay

Shifts small if
Clear, a past become
What it is: detached, seen, despoiling
    Its richnesses.

If ever it
Had them: houses
With love in bed weaning to fullness
    Its moment.

But sun
Puts forth the light
We move on, a track from past
    We leave

Through sea's
Incessant hiss of
Collision on the boat
    As it pushes

Sharp, taut way
On tormenting waters.
If we turned back, what past is
    Preserved through

    Itself would be
Made bare of fact as
A scoured shelf is first deprived
    Of jars

    Then
The skin of dusts
That vaguely obscures the first white
    Cleanness.

    What we fear
Is such past which
Not destroyed yet now falls short
    Of what we were —

    As we move on
Light, a track that leads
From the town shrinking like a heart
    In moral danger.

    Where we lay
And took, as bird
Rising in flames takes
    Victory in pain.

    Only less.
Small but hard the moment
Of indestructible heart.
    Which is burning;

Caught, stilled, held
Through its own pain.
No other terms. Nothing more
    Or smaller

    Allays, increases
Whether or not it
Be burden, or kind of crutches.
    If the boat

    Cuts the sea
It is waters also
Persuade it to cut, clenching us
    The further

    We rise over
The poised lifts high
Of salt rent through which
    The misery

    Pours in,
A weight
With mass without sense
    On, on

    What hope had.
The heart with love.
We have no heart. There is
    Again the moving

    Out from, the pause
On the tip of piled
Waters, the fall, then.
    In departing.

We must be
On, having now
Less than there was: the land
   That we ever

   Constantly held
In belief, a claim
In substance, less now; and we move
   From it. Yet

   There is this:
When the limits of pain,
Ecstasy, glimmer up, showing a frontier,
   A kind of

   Pure hope; pure
Because it cannot
Be chosen, nor be anything
   Other than

   Now what
Despair makes it, neither
Made nor imagined otherwise.
   The kiss on

   Your closed eyes,
If this is despair
As we move from what we knew
   Over water

   We did not
Think as tented, pulled
In such upward wrath of earth,
   Then it also

Is hope; as
Under my kiss you
Ask if this is possible
And I say

Yes, this is possible.

The Wholeness

Tiny stones
Have misery
Unforfeited though bound with
Good roots.

The continual
Sway, deeply rooted,
Of the branches of solitudes
Shares pain.

Stones in
Their large or
Minute splendours, or the olive
That recalls

Its inner
Shape, even
The hand that planted it,
Bring little

To the flesh
With that
Spirit it nurses; we have
Small contact.

This olive,
With the hand
That scooped earth for it; masts of cedars
Poised high

In thought —
This sensuousness
This getting of images
　Was never

Sensuousness,
But handled, merely;
I am a man waiting his dead wife's touch.
　And I wait

As though
This getting of richness,
All unctions of spiced Asia,
　The animal

Oozings of
Gums, salivas
Of odours that leaves yield
　To touching,

Is nothing.
Truly this seems nothing
Compared to the modest touch
　Of the hand

Gently
On cheeks, places
As curved, but laid modestly.
　We did not

Share in this
Touching and yielding,
This courting sensuousness
　Of earth.

If then
I was content,
I should be glorious now.
    I partake

    Of the olive;
I plant and reap;
I have sharing in grinding of
    What I gather.

    Yet having
The harvest I
Do not possess it; it seems
    Its granary

    But not grain.
It is increase
But formally, mine as
    Stones are.

    I therefore
Distrust that past.
Many gathered seeds without issue.
    We walked

    You, the soul,
I, the flesh, speaking
As with finger-tips held up.
    And though we

    Have use
Of these, they
Are as if rented; no man's.
    And they

Stand from
Their wholenesses;
We are two-selved
   Creatures that

   Each with
Self-violation charges
Under the strange, live sun
   Its destruction.

   The tiny stone
Of creation charges
The fluid in the crude oyster that forms
   The pearl. But

   No precious
Creation nor wholeness
Of charged pain beautifully
   Entire

Is of me; I have no commodity.

The infinite charges of the flesh
The commodities of sensuousness,
The olive, pearl, stones of creation —
In their sensuousness these tear us.

   Yet the mental
Forces billow, and joy,
If it is joy, as we are torn
   Quickens you to grow;

Not as
A quick seed in stone
But as you never grew, swellings
   Of wheats,

   And then
The billowing of
The entire meadow of curved stem.
   Silent in

   The stirring
Crop, the predator
Is dismayed, and takes flight.
   I perceive

   Your growth,
In which
Perception plant my grain.
   For I

   Lived before
Through flesh only,
As it were, on some infinite store
   Of images;

   But on these
As the eye
Cannot touch and the hand touches,
   Merely.

   As the seed
Struggles with
Soil to flower with assertions
   Of more seed:

We rear with
The one the other an
Infinite sensuousness of wheat
   In commodity.

   The dying
Body in paroxysm
Turns over: we turn
   Away from

   An older
Disaffection. The branches
Stir above the healed lovers.
   The huge halves

Of this life are one for once.

from _____
Nature
with Man

Nature with Man

The lank summer grass
As it is, bent and wailing;
A scorching wind
Scours a whole plain of it.
Dust still oppresses. Then
As if the earth received
A bruise a pool of brown
Slime erupts slowly
From among the stems. Summer mud . . .
Hot and stagnant. The grass stalks
Stand pricked without root
In the rimless mud . . . in what eye.
On some field of grey stone
A white sud of saliva,
So fine it seems a mildew,
Agonizes over the crop.

But are the humans here? Nature
Had a human head. The mouth
Turned on its long neck, biting through
Scale, sinew; and the blood
Carried through the flesh
Beyond the ends of veins
As the severed head
Rolled into the bullrushes.
This limp and useless
Going off among tall weeds
Has soured the earth, whose body
Decays and perishes.
As for the pain
That suds onto the stone;
That, simply, is pain.

How much else is there?
There is only one head.
But it has several minds
Which still give out
Great reticulations
Of ideas, nets wilful and sharp
Over it; binding it
In pride and thought that cut
The smiling face of pleasure.

'O pity, pity, pity'?
But the weedy soul is shrinking.
Nor can it see how
To join itself unto
The membered flesh. The whole
Of nature is turning slowly
Into an eye that searches
For its most developed
And treacherous creature, man.
Monstrous and huge eye:
The entire process
Of nature perverted
Into the search for him.

Soon

Our boat gorged up
Between shores, whose vines
Held light, pushing it onto
The sea underneath.
Nothing spoke. The cut
Waters spent themselves
Inches between the craft
And close shore. Grapes tangled
With the mast, and fell.
Through a chasm of plants
We emerged, and there,
Wanted breath. Our sides,
And foreheads, creased wetly.
We lived, we knew. And then
Anchored into the space
We came on, without speech.
And of one movement
Went onto land. Through woods
Where dust with green
Spines of fir passed
By the shoe, we climbed.
We came to tilled fields
Whose corn had been grasped,
Or whose nuts, & vines,
Waited a man's hand.
But nowhere was that creature,
His mule not seen. Until
Over a plateau with
Some cypresses we saw

The temple. The queer thing
Between us was the silence
Thinning the air; its clearness
Bore the sun on us.
And here, like flies, we moved
Distractedly, with membranous
Hands raised upwards.
And each of us, I felt,
If he could have believed
Would have spoken; admitting
The cold nourishment of fear.
Fear we had not:
Save for our half-fear
Stronger than all. Tired
Of this I moved up to
A cypress, erect, tapering.
And picked up from the ground,
With fangs open, the ends
Shaped like small clubs,
A cone. I lifted it:
Emissions of seed spilled
Over my hand, infesting
It with seminal decay,
Leaving on the core inside
A speckled whiteness.

Defence

(For Ann)

What 'one-in-five' can do
No man can quite do

She arrived late, with this motto:
'Time used in reconnaissance
Is not time lost.' Useful hint
On how efficient our defences
Would be. Sent from the *Home Office*
On 'Work of some importance'.
And 'The first thing' she said
'Is that there will be four minutes
Of preparation before
The thing is dropped. You should
Instruct persons to stand
In the centre of what room
They like — for the blast,
Unlike the bombs of the previous war,
Will draw the walls out.
There will be no crushing
Of flesh. Instead
On all sides walls will reveal
The citizen unharmed.' Here a question,
But 'No' she said 'we have
From our *Intelligence*
Absolute assurance
Our capital is not targeted.'
Total warfare, by arrangement.

And she was sure, when pressed.
'But there will be devastation
As we now suspect, in radius
Of forty-four miles.
The water will be infected;
The light from the thing, astonishing;
Which though surprised by, we should
Not look at; but shelter
Behind some object "to reduce
Damage to the tissue"
From radiation; or shelter
Under brown paper;
Or, if you can, —
Sheets soaked in urine.'

So women who crotchet, stop that;
Men labouring whose issue is
The two-handed house, set that aside.
Girls big and delicate
With child, turn on your side;
You will melt. The ravelling spider
And the scorpion whose prongs itch
Will fuse in a viscoid
Tar, black as a huge fly.
The whole of nature
Is a preying upon.
Let man, whose mind is large,
Legislate for
All passionate things,
All sensate things: the sensuous
Grass, whose speech is all
In its sharp, bending blade.

Leave not a leaf, a stone
That rested on the dead
To its own dissolution.

She left then,
As if she were with her feet
Turning an enormous,
If man-made, pearl
As means of locomotion.

The Child

Something that can be heard
Is a grasping of soft fingers
Behind that door.
Oh come in, please come in
And be seated.

It was hard to be sure,
Because for some time a creature
Had bitten at the wood.
But this was something else; a pure noise
Humanly shaped

That gently insists on
Being present. I am sure you are.
Look: the pots over the fire
On a shelf, just put;
So, and no other way,

Are as you have seen them; and you,
Being visible, make them no different.
No man nor thing shall take
Your place from you; so little,
You would think, to ask for.

I have not denied: you know that.
Do you? Do you see
How you are guttered
At a breath, a flicker from me?
Burn more then.

Move this way with me,
Over the stone. Here are
Your father's utensils on
The kitchen wall; cling
As I lead you.

It seems you have come without speech,
And flesh. If it be love
That moves with smallness through
These rooms, speak to me,
As you move.

You have not come with
Me, but burn on the stone.

If I could pick you up
If I could lift you;
Can a thing be weightless?
I have seen, when I did lift you

How your flesh was casually
Pressed in. You have come
Without bone, or blood.
Is that to be preferred?
A flesh without

Sinew, a bone that has
No hardness, and will not snap.
Hair with no spring; without
Juices, touching, or speech.
What are you?

Or rather, show me, since
You cannot speak, that you are real;
A proper effusion of air,
Not that I doubt, blown by a breath
Into my child;

As if you might grow on that vapour
To thought, or natural movement
That expresses, 'I know where I am.'
Yet that you are here,
I feel.

Though you are different.
The brain being touched lightly,
It was gone. Yet since you live,
As if you were not born,
Strangeness of strangeness, speak.

Or rather, touch my breath
With your breath, steadily
And breathe yourself into me.

The soft huge pulsing comes
And passes through my flesh
Out of my hearing.

Something has been teased from me

Something has been teased from me
Something insistent and tentative, as grass is
With soil; each binding, each nourishing, both.

We together were like them,
Knit, as the insistent roots of grass compact soil in a field:
A system of thread holding soil it eased into particles.

Their strength crumbles stone:
You allowed penetration. What can't be stopped must be
        nourished —
Pervading like grass, a sort of fire.

That would not quite do.
Grass does not feed itself, soil is bound by roots.
It is a composure the grass gives. You asked

For some change in me; insisted.
You shrilled, were acrid to the touch; but grass cannot
        change its roots.
It seeds itself in the soil, needing it; but is not soil.

My roots offended:
That tentative strength from which I pushed
Tall, seeded, sharp; whose webbed anchorage held you.

What could I have done?
I was loathed for what I was best, filled
You with liquids not yours. I seemed not good for you.

And slowly, I became
Undesired. What you needed,

You stopped me being:
A thing that cracked stone, ate it by means of roots.
I became reed delicate, a set of porous fibres.

It is not natural to
Grow by separation.

We did.
We pressed each other off, and grew through that.

The fruited thing persists.
It is corded, and thickly braided, like the unopened
        bluebell's flower.
It grows in you. It demands shape and blood
As it thickens to consciousness.

A single thickening sharpness lifts
Through moisture. It is nearly to be tolerated;
It has to be. A part of me fastens in you.

Grass sucks water and salts in,
As if it alone existed. This thing is more swollen.
But it is grass I think this bone and blood

Is like, persisting as grass, a blade of bone and flesh
Lifting to consciousness. It integrates
Into a flexible and feeling flesh.

As you lie down to
Give it its way, you turn on your side, lifting up
Your right thigh, shaped like dropping moisture, to your
      breast.

      It demands strength
From you. Heaves. You heave. It is coming away.
It is good; it is to be endured.

      It has to be. It comes away,
And as it does is given breath.
Milk trickles through the tubules.
It lies beside you, put there. It will cry out.

      And be nourished by you.
And grow like grass, wastefully. For now,
You hold it in your arms, and nurture it.

Flower Poems

Dandelion

Slugs nestle where the stem
Broken, bleeds milk.
The flower is eyeless: the sight is compelled
By small, coarse, sharp petals,
Like metal shreds. Formed,
They puncture, irregularly perforate
Their yellow, brutal glare.
And certainly want to
Devour the earth. With an ample movement
They are a foot high, as you look.
And coming back, they take hold
On pert domestic strains.
Others' lives are theirs. Between them
And domesticity,
Grass. They infest its weak land;
Fatten, hide slugs, infestate.
They look like plates; more closely
Like the first tryings, the machines, of nature
Riveted into her, successful.

A Bluebell

Most of them in the first tryings
Of nature, hang at angles,
Like lamps. These though
Look round, like young birds,

Poised on their stems. Closer,
In all their sweetness, malevolent. For there is
In the closed, blue flower, gas-coloured,
A seed-like dark green eye.
Caraway, grained, supple,
And watching; it is always there,
Fibrous, alerted,
Coarse grained enough to print
Out all your false delight
In 'sweet nature'. This is struggle.
The beetle exudes rot: the bee
Grapples the reluctant nectar
Coy, suppurating, and unresigned.
Buds print the human passion
Pure now not still immersed
In fighting wire worms.

Lilies of the Valley

Minute flowers harden. Depend
From thin bowing stem;
Are white as babies' teeth.
With broad leaves, immobile;
Are sheath-like, and fat.
What have these to do with beauty?
They must take you with
A fingering odour, clutches the senses,
Fills the creases and tightens the wind's seams,
As noise does. The plant is equipped.
Even then you don't like it.
Gradually though

Its predatory scent
Betters you, forces you, and more than
The protected rose creating
A sculptured distant adulation
For itself. This insinuates, then grapples you,
Being hungry; not poised, not gerundive.
Hard, and uncrushed, these flowerheads;
Like beads, in your palm.
You cannot destroy that conquering amorousness
Drenches the glands, and starts
The belled memory. Glows there, with odour.
Memorable as the skin
Of a fierce animal.

Peonies

It has a group of flowers.
Its buds shut, they exude
A moisture, a gum, expressed
From the sepals' metallic pressures.
Its colour shows between shields,
Cramped where the long neck
Swells into the head. Then they open.
They do it gradually,
Stammer at first. It is a confidence
Permits this; push aside
The shield, spray outwards,
Mount in height and colour
Upon the stem.
They claim the attention up there.
The focus of all else. Not aloof at all;

Brilliantly intimate,
They make the whites of others
A shrunk milk. They must draw
To them, the male ardours,
Enthusiasms; are predatory
In seeking them. Obliterate the garden
In flickerless ease, gouging out
The reluctant desires. Theirs is one rule,
And is found everywhere
Feeling transpires — extends
Its tendrils, helplessly grappling for
Passion of a different order
Than the peonies'.
What will be looked at,
However fleshily adequate,
Conquers the amorous.
By nature, a devourer. Cannot give.
Gives nothing.
In winter shrinks to a few sticks,
Its reversion, bunches of hollowness.
Pithless. Insensate, as before.

The Strawberry Plant

The rootless strawberry plant
Moves across the soil. It hops
Six inches. Has no single location,
Or root.
You cannot point to its origin,
Or parent. It shoots out
A pipe, and one more plant

Consolidates its ground.
It puts out crude petals, loosely met.
As if the business of flowering
Were to be got over. Their period is brief.
Even then, the fruit is green,
Swart, hairy. Its petals invite tearing
And are gone quickly,
As if they had been. The fruit swells,
Reddens, becomes succulent.
Propagation through the devouring
Appetite of another.
Is sweet, seeded, untruculent;
Slugs like it, all over.
It is nubile to the lips,
And survives even them. And teeth,
Insane with edible fury,
Of the loving kind.

A Daisy

Look unoriginal
Being numerous. They ask for attention
With that gradated yellow swelling
Of oily stamens. Petals focus them:
The eye-lashes grow wide.
Why should not one bring these to a funeral?
And at night, like children,
Without anxiety, their consciousness
Shut with white petals;

Blithe, individual.

The unwearying, small sunflower
Fills the grass
With versions of one eye.
A strength in the full look
Candid, solid, glad.
Domestic as milk.

In multitudes, wait,
Each, to be looked at, spoken to.
They do not wither;
Their going, a pressure
Of elate sympathy
Released from you.
Rich up to the last interval
With minute tubes of oil, pollen;
Utterly without scent, for the eye,
For the eye, simply. For the mind
And its invisible organ,
That feeling thing.

The Violet

The lobed petals receive
Each other's nestling shape.

We share the sun's beneficence:
Frost, men, snowdrops.
Then the violet unfolds. Not an uncasing
Of the corolla, each petal compliant
To the purpose of survival, obedient to that; but as it feels
The sun's heat, that puberty

Pushes out from its earlier self-clasping
Two distinct, clenched halves. Stiffens them.
These fluttering portions that made
The bud, separately elect
To be the flower; the violet
Halves itself, pushing apart
In two separate forces;
It divides up itself, it becomes two violet portions.
It is not a conformation of members,
Each petal a tooth, an eyelash.
On the other hand, the violet is torn apart.
Its increase is by dividing;
Its stiffened petals push further apart.
It adheres to its nature; it has no maturity,
Other than this.
It requires courage, and finds that
In this unclasping of its self-worship: two palms tentatively
Open. Going both ways,
They absorb a huge circle
Of violeted air, an intent
Movement of embrace;
Created, exposed, powerful.
The air is coloured somewhat violet.
It costs itself much.

Milkmaids
(Lady's Smock)

Ridging the stalk's length,
The pith ducts. You'd think
The leaves found by water. Their openness

Guards them; a giddy, a careless
Effusion of stem. That is strength.
From the topmost, a flower triumphs.
From each undomestic
Flare, four petals; thrown wide; a flexible
Unplanned exuberance.
A veined fat is under
The svelte integument;
A kind of vegetative warmth.
From the centre, axial, determined
Extend the stamens, long by usage
For survival, and grouped
Round the curt stigma. Nothing less enslaved,
Less domestic to man, they are twice free.
Will wander through your plot in whole families.
You will not cut milkmaids down.

That tender, that wild, strength
Sucks the untrammelled consciousness up.
They mount the incline breathless
Pale violet. Their eyes wide,
They halt at the wire. This is the camp.
In silent shock a multitude of violet faces
Their aghast petals stiff, at the putrescence
Of the crowd wired up. This halts them:
The showing bone; the ridges of famine,
Protrusions, want, reduction.
Silent also, they confront with their modesty
Of demeanour — the stiff fatigue
Of the sack jackets something altogether different
From those who supervise
In their soft, rigid cloth —

The prisoners confront
The unservanted faces of the plants.

Between their silences, comprehension; like the wire
Halted, staked, live.
Crowding through the tented cloth
That locust death, to each person.
For the flowers, the forked,
Upright sense of human
Creatures wanting patience, pulped, compounded into
    their children.

Moss

'Patents' will burn it out; it would lie there
Turning white. It shelters on the soil; quilts it.
So persons lie over it; but look closely:
The thick, short green threads quiver like an animal
As a fungoid quivers between that and vegetable:
A mushroom's flesh with the texture and consistency of
    a kidney.

Moss is soft as a pouch.
There are too many shoots though, boxed compacted,
Yet nestling together,
Softly luminous.
They squirm minutely. The less compact kind
Has struggling white flowers; closed,
Like a minute bell's clapper;
So minute that opened then, its stretch seems wide.
The first grows in damper places.

With what does it propagate?
Quiet, of course, it adheres to
The cracks of waste-pipes, velvets,
Velours them; an enriching
Unnatural ruff swathing the urban 'manifestation':
The urban nature is basemented, semi-dark;
It musts, it is alone.

Here moss cools; it has no children;
It amplifies itself.
Could that over-knit fiction of stubbed threads reproduce
Defined creatures?
It hovers tentatively between one life and another,
Being the closed-road of plants,
Its mule; spreads only its kind —
A soft stone. It is not mad.
Reared on the creeping dankness of earth
It overspreads, smears, begrudges something
Though it is passive; spreads wildly.
It is immune to nothing;
You cannot speak of misery to it.

Crowfoot (in water)

It is found, rooted,
In still water. A leaf,
Shaped like a kidney, floats
Leafing the underside of air, over water,
Taking in both, each side.
Inside the water
Are filaments of flesh-thread

Hair-drifting.
The flowers are white,
Simple, articulate.
Nothing smutches them.
Mouths of cattle, large
As sycamore trees,
Eat and compact stalk,
Leaf, stigma, and pigment
Into their food.

Shapes that no flower bred,
Not like any contour of nature,
Are piece-mealed
To a sponge of surging parts.

Articulate plant-speech does smutch
The ridged palate, bellying towards
The organ of hunger, minutely impotent.
The chopped articulation in the throat, —
Cattle's throat, — the woe
Is devoured. Crowfeet concerts
Its parts in a webbed cry.

If ripe, the seeds rear in
Dung casually dropped.

The rest persists under
The pond's rim. Can be devoured
To an inch of its life.

Harebell

The harebell is one flower,
Its solitariness
Bespoke by its colour, not blue
Nor violet; hovering between, precisely.
It is a spare delicate bell.
Inside it are three pale sugary stigmas welded
To each other at equal angles,
Not seen until looked for.
Its stem is thin as wire.
The flower looks down, and if
Lifted, looks fixedly
At the admirer.
Its silence halted between primness and beauty,
Its shape is wrung from the sounds of life round it
As a bell's sound forms the bell's shape from silence,
And resumes its demure integrity;
More precise, more shaped, than the bluebell;
More venturesome. More stirred, ungarrulous.
Stern as a pin.

from _____
Amana Grass

Six Cemetery Poems

1

In Iowa, we rested, seeing on a rib of ground behind a
                                                lighted field
a minute cemetery, without church. Flowers lie at the
                                        heads of lengths of turf
held motionless by the dead; flowers at the neckline of
                                        headstones chipped or not.
Of twenty, cared for, half were lopped, the material token
hacked where, below, the neckline was profusely tended.
Through cut grass roots of trees rise, at the surface
                                burnished by feet, or by a roller.
The dead's place, combed here, and decked, by lively
                                                        hands.
They are present, you said; why, if such force passes
                                between your body and mine?
as the record plays, does your hand open my lips again?
what figures does the mirror keep
and the camera secrete of what the eye and it took?
These have died. I said: that woman remembers her
                                                        daughter
quickened by her above ground.
I am not consoled, you said.
I want to keep your form which holds my flesh from bone
                                                to bone, open.
I am holding in me the breath of the dead; their breath,
                                                        only.

2

From the road, I saw a small, rounded bluff, a cemetery
tufted on it, churchless, and squarely contained by wire
                                                        fencing;

one more field, increasing in it a short, thick tree.
Its branches emerged, multiplying densely, compacting
an opaque bud of wood and leaves not chinking
light through, or air; populous of itself, impacted.
It had been planted among the dead, or grew
with them, first there perhaps, the dead
put about the tree, in urban grid-like plots.
Since void, that had tissue and bone from them disjoined
into bland nitrogens the tree burgeons in.
Burgeons and thickens, the graves tidied
emptily on its root-veined lumpy wildness;
the graves in distinguishable order,
their territorial bitterness lapsing
into the dense acid wood. Lingeringly
it darkens, and I feel the headstones' life
lengthening past the deads' lives, or any trim, lively care.
The stones split into the shape
the roots strain under with gregarious presence.
The fence's tension snaps, with the grid's.

3

he made the rampart and the wall lament;
they languished together
                    Lamentations 2, viii

The face, in several sweet bones, fitted,
to her skull's, the bones shaped into its form, is fleshed
                                        in joy
delighting in itself which issues joy, joyous to feel.
The hair congruous and abundant from pleasure springs
down her face to her knees, her legs folded beneath her,
                    the hair, its grieving length,

over the floor. I expect your cry.
A tree, as if its branches are of hair, bends
these, trailing them to its necessary pool. Stops there.
The hair of the tree fluxes to water.
Your hair, in branchfuls, the tree-shape
bends and flows through your face: the tree
in its all-eyed shape nurtured
by the untearful pool
shedding no jot of itself.
Where is the reciprocal shedding
from the faces, working in grief, the one for the other,
or between even you and me; your hurt
working its face from mine,
your tear in a metal-like
leaf, tugging, at the eye of him who'd weep, for the one
                                    weeping herself.
Nothing weeps here that does not weep, for itself, alone,
the tough small disc of grief
shuddering the body, the joyful hair leaping
like water to the ground in a cry.

4

In Anamosa sandstone is cut for a prison by men from
                                    Iowa.
Space fits where stone was, at its top a tree hangs its naked
                                    root through.
Below, they are sawing blocks; at the saw's teeth, nerves
                                    catch;
and skin, and hair at the fore arm, and dust, congeal with
                                    sweat
a mucous not sensitive to its own touch. Slits in
the jail walls sense a division of light straiter than a chapel's.

As much width as the weeping judicial eye admits
of light at its mind. The prison honours the free men,
who work earth for corn. Here's a farm, a grain barn,
and at the limits of it, staked, a cemetery, every man
that is here on his feet. No weight of stone
keeps the man under earth, or headstone attributes
him. A stone column its head shrunk to it, a skull
bevelled and elongated, each as the next is, without
ornament, and no jot of name. No burial has been here,
earth cut, flesh wrapped, and the soil again heaped
on the flesh as though you felt it upon your own.
Each grave is uniform in the signification of death:
no grub hatches at where the flesh turns putrid, no smell
of flesh softly green insinuates the haired nostrils.
I feel the garb of each man's life, erect, obedient,
and stronger than the death of his body.

5

It has taken breath, but of that it seems to have none.
As though it had drawn breath and died, that, and its cage
now, stiffened.
The grass bank swelled, is swelled and though rigid, is glad,
an unadorned joy falling slowly across the incline,
that has yet being dead a winsome thing to offer.
On it neither flower nor beast, unless a man, treads
but in the rising, then flatness the slope bends into, mostly
glad.
And at the crown, a house, not joyful, holds
in place that fluid continuous pleasure the ground
though dead does not hold back. As a man keeps
place with the peaceable, austere beasts he is disarmed by.
The house, in wood and white, shimmers, it dances

the government house, ample and consolidated, jigs —
in foreign substance timbered into American earth,
various and fraternal. American Indians
dwindled into margins of plain flat under
bison with their bent horn the Indian must have,
that the white men bulleted. In Iowa
a cemetery is planted out and fenced on the town's
                                          margins,
square and strict, newish, the Jews', federated
as the wars demanded, or age did; the Jewish American
dead in earth, in rows, neat, decked with small limp flags.
In form, native; breathless, voided into the fecund
corn-belt, wanting memory: doctors, farm-men, dead
                                          soldiers

merged with clart particles of soil
that can't grasp spaces until wormed
by flesh that's American, dead, preponderant
and exalted. The others are scattered
boneless, and wearied of their individual substance
blent and lost near the cemented onrush of crank-ridden
                                          highway,
the fast interstate mindfully pressed
between two steep flanks of heavy soil,
one dwindling slowly to the cemetery, a loose iron gate to
                                          it,
foundling, amnesiac, the most recent.

6

for Paul Tracy

Miners dead inside coal seamed by fire, under Pittsburgh
or between lead, from poison that touched and made stiff
the liver as it opened last: what the flesh failed of
employment caused. Prospectors, their wives, and issue
come of wiving, they are each dead
who obsessed, impregnated, and made the retina
gravid with images of silver.
I found evidence of them on a hill below
where the cage had ceased; no church by them, or metal.
I found more dead, fewer though, near a canyon
named Sucker Creek, east from that, and in
a field, the green square it contained staked with posts
erect at the corners, holding wire up.
Few dead, where few were living, and against
their solitary gentleness, or brutality, as some
fetched a tendon to their neighbours' throats, a farm cart
with four large wheels, its shafts erect, dark red
and stiff above the wire its carcase
is tethered at; living carcase; the arms
raised in astonishment, and fixed
at joints stuck now. Perpetually agape.
Together, the dead are crustacean, the large
crab of the soil, pincering its track under
earth that will fracture, webbed by micturating roots
dregging earth of its nutriment. The dead heave it open
and move with vulnerable hugeness on it.
A four legged slowness that is a limp almost.
I hear each ligament and tendon working
to print back on us what we let them have

as they aged and sickened. I am afraid
of the jointed, vulnerable, crab-wise dead.
The cemetery waits, contemptuously patient
at their congealed practice. Listless crust about soft flesh.
The cart's arms jar, their load to be re-assumed.

from Amana Grass

The leaf of your hand shall touch but not cover me
New England proverb

Amana grass, its spikes of hair rayed as branches
from long stems, is sucked by three locomotives, their haul
filling space over tracks. Wind wraps its length,
hot and dieseled, through spaces of stumpy grass, barely
green
over long slight inclines. Air in varying pressures blowing
on the train
sounds fiercely between houses, where space, holding
other spaces, of human loneliness, meshes.
The same in that wildness locomotives haven't seen;
beneath earth filaments of root, everything, tangle.
The train links points in which the human crouches,
is found, rejoices. Wind appears to feel out crevice,
and surface. Does not feel, no pain at all in how it contacts.
The sun's light, without visible sun, sinks coldly through
frigid wind.
A leaf turns upon asphalt treading through the park.
Wind picks at a face rising and sinking on long legs
stockinged, their tan rushing to compare with the net's
colour.
Nearing, she seems to compose her face, the air being
frigid.
Slim, as the legs are, almost a woman's; not fleshy yet, or
coy now
the thighs swelling behind a skirt now short, the hips
larger than they were, composed, each, into tentative
prominence

the mild fury she receives of her intent frail hulk.
Of the mid-west, in bulk, solemn, a flat grandeur under its
                                        heights of corn,
she strains little to her. Of what is there,
a train's horn contracting desolating space.
Of what she is, something ribbed; of what she has, nearing,
the rib enlarged. Of who she'll be,
the clasp that broaches two minds, hasn't enjoined them.
The face's sadness, tenacious shadow, melts into resolution.
Speak louder; shout, for I should hear,
the wind asks, each creature begged of it.
Each thing is to its need, not much remaining to implore.
Space the train threads grasps for more; in it, a tree
shakes leaves rustlingly at grasses naming them sharp
                                        stump.
Grass tightens fierce roots on fractions of soil.
The soil, from stone, in passivity, grins; is to ingest all.
How, among nature's divine egotisms, to grow
her especial fronds, antennae sensible to another.
To enlarge, amid these natures, whose heraldic egotisms
                                        silently conflict,
she must fight. Earth's fullness, though,
may be shared; fleshy needs, feathery demands, requited
'among the stained emblems under which the stiffened
                                        flesh
fragments. On the bits, vultures perch that, gleaming
on frozen blood as if armour mirroring the dead enemy's
                                        conquest, rip the flesh
their image flares on, captive since to what they strip,
flesh, not stubborn or curious.' Brown grass ends are as
                                        limp,
and thinned, as crystals of falling snow are intense:

experienced and dense, the aged spirit sheds itself.
Appear in the air, edged; bitter against nostrils and
                                      cheekbone.
Wind stirs it onto each creature unremembering of earlier
                                      needs
to be required by what creeps and grins against its knots.
She tightens her coat onto her breasts, scarf lightly to her
                                      ears.
She'll get home. He moves through it, sure he'll find her;
white powders, some of heaven's properties, sift over the
                                      sidewalk
bonily cramping the foot inside its strict shoe.
Treading he sees in virgin snow someone's feet printed
towards her house, before him, his, exactly. Snow
lifts into his face, melting flakes caught in clenched
                                      eyelashes,
blasted on edge to him it is adrenalin charging
the mind's eye to dilate over the prints. Calmness
then. He turns, from tracked eddies of feet past
her house, to her, feeling for her ornate small key.
The evening star, in fruitful magnificence, rises with
        moistening splendour, towards the sky's taut,
                                      precise limits.
He approaches, the counterpane unpuckered, smooth for
                the crushing of heedless, fruitful weight.
No evening meal. Thought of food prepared by each one
broken down, as if by enzyme, into other hunger.
Pancakes nurtured into floury presence; stay-in-bed hash;
                                      sauce
biting its butterscotchings sweetly into cream and cake;
                                      these, gone.
Her lips parted as if breath, passing between, stirred the
                loose hair shaking past the forehead,

she summons the first kiss to her body. He parts her lips,
                              his tongue stiffened into her.
The spirit dilates; the fleshy circlet starts its flow.
Older, he prepares: on his breast heraldries of self-power
                                        chevalring love
stain him: on her breasts, prints of the stain.
He presses her down, she helping him, parts her, and
                                        enters.
She won't move. Forced to him, and pinned, she can't.
The spike piercing the belt that holds it as it stiffens
upon the bar; tightened upon each other
so he in her, so she round him. Malely and femalely
they are clung by self-swellings they can't slip
of a sexual love ending in each other's
mirroring vauntedness. 'For whom do I brag?'
Then stricken to tenderness, minted, as if to the doe's
                                        hunter,
he askes of her: 'Did we make this, of our intent hungers?'
She fears it may be worse. She, feeling pure, the dew might
                                        look
sullied. The purities in her chill, condensing her heat
to drops that lustre her success, or, if she fails, rebuke her
that she melted in her their dewy script that in
unsweatlike nature gleams through the skin of women.
He gets off her, hot and distanced; she faces up to the
                                        ceiling;
her thighs are separate in distress and coldness.
Flat Iowa is stretched in snow, through which her
                                Vermont hills rise
strict as her mother's breast, wrinkling the torn flats they
                                        break.
Her nipples lose their stiffness, her breasts not thickening
                                        a milk

should have milk were a hand on them, smaller than his.
A strict, sweet whiteness, purely of her breasts
is, for her, the milk achingly sucked by her child's lips.
Unlike her vaginal whitenesses, or a man's sperm, flukelike
at her itch; her breasts' exclusion, each one.
He turns from position onto his back. Wind like pricking
                                      metal
over the surface of another exclaims a passion
length-like as the scoring on him of hair naked.
Like the pressure of touch, the wind's, her hair scrapes her
                                      silence
through him its length. It is to him as to a beast
that working four he puts a hundred feet down
to his mile of hillside's inch.
Her silence teases her apart, forming distance, cars
slithering from each other. She separate, he distanced.
It is England's width, soon, the north part, stone,
where the silver mine fills, on chipped quartz, chipped
                              limestone, earth, wire,
lies, at any rate, choked, — the plants at this segment of
                              earth's carefully spun rim
rubbed small, low, wiry, red; car-rush whirring such
                              colour
rearward of the mind, darkening, with the sun melting
through north England, its heights, flat as Iowa's,
dark, extinct, which he travels. — As she moves away
to Vermont's hills, shrunk, folding as they cooled
into claustral heights, wooded though, familial. . . .

. . . . I need the image of you bearable
by control, and within my courage;
or my courage to grow, matching that quick in you

paying out the veined, the thin, lines
of your shape in durable contour.
But that is exacting. So the thing I want
is that you with the passionate elegance of a beast
into the man's love breathe yours; in age, holding
your value to your body, move, as you must,
in some reluctance, to your death.
— A night past I dreamt of the hire purchase man
asleep with his wife; both seemed young and pliant.
They lay naked; his arms clasping her waist,
his head rested between her supple breasts.
I saw that he dreamt, and what it was;
not of his wife, or of some other deeply
moulded eager girl. Belshazzar-like
he dreamed that, fanged, he, on hands and knees, crept
with open salivating jaws on the poor
and negroes, lively victims, in his right hand
the papers of his wealth-to-be laced
with the strictures, bonds, enforcements that would
                                            ligament
them to him. His wife stood naked
and grinning among us, papering the ink-smeared
visible body with signed bonds,
but mostly, about her cunt, she pressed
the papers, wadding and girding her fruitful organs,
shutting her sex from view, and access. This was
her assent, her husband's dream, and my containment.
I was speaking of love, and America; and how
I value it, as I knew you did,
when you wrote: 'I want to be a woman
to a man so badly, I can taste it almost.'
I was speaking of value, I guess. Of what

knits in the spaces, where wind
creases its frigid movements into the face
as it swerves on. I was speaking of you,
and of love once more: warm, intelligenced, exacting;
of more immanent value than Hebrew parallelism
or the Anglo-Saxon metre.

A Word about Freedom and Identity in Tel-Aviv

Through a square sealed-off with
a grey & ornate house,
its length bent, for one corner of that,
a road leads off, got to down steps:
wide, terraced, ample.
The road's quiet, too; but nudges as
the square did not. Walking
some, below the city I heard
a pared, harsh cry, sustained
and hovering, between outrage
and despair; scraped by itself
into a wedge-shape opening on
inaccessibly demented hurt
it can't since quite come at;
imitative, harsh, genuine.
A pet-shop four feet below
pavement level; in its front yard
a blue parrot, its open beak
hooked and black, the folded wings
irregularly lifting a little;
under which, dull yellow soft plumage,
the insides of itself, heaved, slightly.
Its tail was long, stiff. Long in stiffness
that at once bends entirely
if bent too much. And as it
turned in its cage, bending the tail
against the wires, it spoke
into the claw it raised
at its hooked face, the word
'torah, torah' in the hoarse, devotional

grief religious men speak with
rendering on God the law
their love binds them with. Done,
it cried its own cry, its claws tightening
onto its beak, shaking slowly
the whole face with the cry
from side to side. This cry was placed
by one Jew inside another. Not belonging though;
an animal of no distinct race,
its cry also human, slightly;
wired in, waiting; fed on
good seed a bit casually
planted. Granulated, sifted,
dry. The torah is:
suffering begets suffering, that is.

The Torah consists of the body of Jewish religious knowledge.

Jaffa, and Other Places

Toward Jaffa, foot-dragged sand is flattened, and pathed,
                         the hardened grains
fusing then to a road, on which the fallen foot stifles.
                 Houses shake into dereliction.
A flat incohering of sand with bricks, remaining feet
                        above, stays.
A gulley cuts through these levels down, sprains in its
                        sides, between
which pours brick, charred wood, tarpaulin, stopped.
                     Inertia heaps:
mound of boots, motionless and brown, remains of the
             mandate army, dispersed in England now.
Done with in worse places: shoes, crutches, irons, many
    oddments, each similar, the inert teeth, ash, hair, dust
winnowed between grains of soil or not winnowed
                    between them;
most of each category useful, separated. The flesh gets
                  isolated from these,
the goods and its body harrowed apart. Each item heaps
                         on
one of its kind, itself buried. Wardresses help sort each
                     class.
And not the negro, his hunted skin finding each shadow
                  not as dark as he
offers an absence as blank. Shortly the spider
is trained to bite at the organ; the bone round it liquefies,
                    the lips
of it attendant and limp. The Reich's swollen architecture
                 will be less dank.
New immigrants near this ashy zone, pacified and burnt.

Divisions

Cedars from Lebanon, in community, move into the swart,
                                                            pointed hills.
I don't say many. On two legs bound into one,
rooted into terraces between drops of rock-face, in sparse
                                                                        soils
cornered where wind pushed that. Layers of snapping
                                                    pointed stone shift,
one can guess, like whelpings, about their roots.
These roots know what they are about. The trees came
                                together; tall, fleshed like a wax feather,
their leaves green throughout. And as the sun changes the
                                                    trees don't; sharp, slim.
Not many know what sex these creatures are made of.
The whole tree comes into the folded integral hills
of Judah, one of many, towards a sea struggling
to erode from the land its form into the shape of Africa.
Creatures with two legs come, and sit against a Cedar that
                                                            no longer moves
forward. They spread a map over their legs, engross a
                                                                    frontier;
a document embossed by lines that divide one bit of land
                                                            from the same bit,
the first of these trees from the last of them. The line is
arbitrary as a fish-hook. As if two iron hooks
stuck like picks into the ground, and their shafts pulled,
until in the earth a gap opened. A small, neat structure of
                                                                        stones,
in fact, marks the hostile step which it is death to step.
Judah's hills do not stoop, they are said to skip; those trees

in Lebanon do not bend; their mild, emulsive
sharpnesses advance through the nourishing earth they
                                        compact.
A hexagon of dirt is trapped back by a leaf into the soil.
Suddenly the landscape, one might say, is startled by
a man in a blue shirt, its greens, its ochres fixed by a depth
                                        of blue;
as if before these changed but now were frozen by the
                        quality of blue that they are not.
He crouches; what is he speaking to the wrinkled olive;
                                what disdain
for the tree's agedness as the plucked creature furs its oil
                        on his salt fingers?
The hills shimmer; also, the tree standing in them: a
                        trembling on one
point from inside. A haze, in dots, condenses over the
                        contracted earth.
Past that tree, there, that shorter one, two men are dead.
The sun is pushing off, the trees persist inside their shade
eating deeply on the earth. Opening the clothes you see
among the groiny hair, the useful penis, in the heat
                        distended slightly.
One of the men's has a head, circumcised; a chin, a ridge
that visibly hardened as its body's blood gathered to it
                                intently.
Alive, a bit of marble with a ruff of skin, in folds; thin,
                        brown, slack.
The other man's is hooded. Each had its fissure that as it
                                entered it
the lips folded back upon themselves, the ground
                        moistening its entrance.
Now the vulva, slightly swollen, its hair local, remains
                        closed however.

The lips closed, in a pained sleep: the female part
                                    ruminant.
No: the female part mourns the unique instrument it was
                                                to it.
The faces of the men show that death, which each divided
                                    on the other's
body, entered the left ear, and then the mouth. In leisure.
None attends them. The sabbath intervenes like a blade.

Worm

Look out, they say, for yourself.
The worm doesn't. It is blind
As a sloe; its death by cutting,
Bitter. Its oozed length is ringed,
With parts swollen. Cold and blind
It is graspable, and writhes
In your hot hand; a small snake, unvenomous.
Its seeds furred and moist
It sexes by lying beside another,
In its eking conjunction of seed
Wriggling and worm-like.
Its ganglia are in its head,
And if this is severed
It must grow backwards.
It is lowly, useful, pink. It breaks
Tons of soil, gorging the humus
Its whole length; its shit a fine cast
Coiled in heaps, a burial mound, or like a shell
Made by a dead snail.
It has a life, which is virtuous
As a farmer's, making his own food.
Passionless as a hoe, sometimes, persistent.
Does not want to kill a thing.

Flatfish

1

It moves vertically through salted
Pressures, with a head that sees sideways.
The nets are submerged, which it enters.
Nothing to come for specially. Men want it.

The white flesh powered by a tail filmed with skin
Sways its mild hulk into their fold.
The white flesh is food. When boiled,
It flakes easily off the bone.

Is this love? God created us
For the toothed shark, the molestation
Of two jaws hinged through flesh
Onto each other's hooked teeth.

Its ethics are formal, determined.
Otherwise He made the mild flatfish,
And gleaning mackerel that flatten
On the dead's helplessness strengthening its rancid colours.

He made the flatfish, their eyes
Naive as a bead drawn from a leopard's skin.
Their white flesh is flaked into the mossy,
Acidic belly, just hanging.

The good salt, phosphate, each dissolved
Into flesh. The fish are left to gasp
In ships' holds, mulcting the air
For air moving in the gill's membrane

Miserly, useless. A gradual pain
Until the fish weaken. Could they cry
We might gas them to concert
Their distress. Nets are men's media,

Their formal, knotted, rectangular intelligence.
They survive on what the fish weighs, their welfare
Accurate as a pair of scales.

2

   We are not going to change.
But husband the sea, planting the fish spawn in
     The frigid heft of plot-water
       Grey, but not stone.

   Mackerel will gorge
A sea parsley, its flowers sprinkled in a white, granular
                                petal;
     The shark will eat mud
       At the sea's foundation.

   Though to reap will be by net,
As many fish as grains husked from their flattened case,
     The ear raped of its oval bolus
       Folded into itself.

   The precise allotment of fish
A growth in kind; pollination by a brush tasked
     Onto differing species
       For the flesh's good.

The flesh's good. Elsewhere
We seized on our own kind, not for food. Each fish
    Glides through a forest,
      An oily lung

Of sea weed, the swell
Moved in a land-grafted integument of sea plant. A
                                  uniform
    Thicket moon-masted, its foliage
      Begins to lock

Fast with sea-forester's
Skill. We evolve with our hands and brain. The pad of each
    Hand, moist; the nails sharp
      As a grown fin.

from

The Principle
of Water

Killhope Wheel

Tree

Under the yard, earth could enable nothing, nothing
opened in it. I smelt it once, when the floor
was up, disabled, rank. I made boxes
and grow mint, rhubarb, parsley
and seedlings that lift a furl of leaves, slightly
aside an unwavering stem.
A friend dragged a barrel off rocks, we took it home;
I chose a tree for it. It is five foot
with branches that may stretch across
the wall, with minute fruits, of hardly any colour.
Its leaves point open, and down. The whole tree
can glisten, or die. It is dark green
in earth mixed with peat dug by a lake
and dung I crumbled in.
I can't fudge up a relationship, but it gladdens
you, as the sun concentrates it, and I
want the creature for what it is
to live beyond me.

(Untitled)

Small hills, among the fells, come apart from the large
where streams drop; the water-flowers
bloom at the edges, or in the shallows, together,
and are white. Whoever comes here, comes, glad, at least
and as they look, it is with some care, you can feel

that on flower, may tree, or dry-stone wall
their gaze collects in a moist, comely pressure.
I feel this, but slog elsewhere.
Swan Hunter's is where we build naval craft;
they emerge: destroyer, the submarine
fitted, at length, by electricians. Their work
is inspected; it is again re-wired. In the heat
men walk high in the hulk on planks, one
of them tips, and he falls the depth of the hold.
It is hot. The shithouses are clagged, the yard's
gates closed for security. The food is not good.
Some people in here are maimed.
I am trying to make again the feeling
plants have, and each creature has, looked at,
demure, exultant. The man who has fallen
looks at me, and looks away.

Centering

At the West End, a bridge.
Coaling houses, shutes, and among such power,
contrived, at the top, a little lever
which would unclasp the heavy trap.
All the ships come for here is fuel. Few come.
And none, further.
Near the bridge, each side, houses
struggling to cross over.

More east, seawards, a further bridge.
The trains bend that way, then, turning square,
cross the whole river.
Below, the quay, meant to focus
activity to it.

The maritime offices, craft
moored from Denmark.
The masts' shadows stable on the customs sheds.

No centre can be formed
here or by the next bridge. The trains
pass on a tier above the road.

Nor here; the road belts between
the strength of the region fused into two spans,
gone.

Two precipitate banks, where water pushes
within a moment of the quick of you, bituminous
and rank.
If you were made
at the river-side
you have to be a spanning, at least.

Killhope Wheel, 1860, County Durham

1860. Killhope Wheel, cast
forty feet in iron across, is swung
by water off the North Pennines
washing lead ore crushed here.

And mined, here. Also fluor-spar.
In 1860 soldiers might kill
miners if they struck.

A board says that we're free to come in.
Why should it seem absurd to get
pain from such permission? Why have

I to see red-coat soldiers prick
between washed stones, and bayonets
tugged from the flesh?

Among the North Pennines what might
have seeped the flesh of miners, who chucked
their tools aside?

I can't work out what I have
come here for; there's no mineable lead
or work of that kind here now.

Why does a board, tacked to wood,
concerning my being free to visit
nourish my useless pain?

Like water. I am its water, dispersed
in the ground I came from; and have footage
on these hills, stripped of lead,

which the sheep crop, insensibly white.
The mist soaks their cries into them.

Strike

The earth comes moist-looking, and blackens;
a trickle of earth where the feet pressed,
twice a day, wearing off the grass.

Where the miners
were seen: a letter blown damply
into the corner of a hut: 'Oh dear love, come to me'
and nothing else.

Where are they?
The sheep bleat back to the mist balding
with terror; where
are they? The miners
are under the ground.

A pale blue patch of thick worsted
a scrag of cotton;
the wheel is still that washed the pounded ore.
They were cut down.

Almost turned by water, a stammer of the huge wheel
groping at the bearings.
Their bayonets; the red coat
gluey with red.

The water shrinks
to its source. The wheel,
in balance.

Spade

George Culley, Isaac Greener?

A want of sound hangs
in a drop of moisture from the wheel that
turned and washed the ore.

A rustling of clothes on the wind. The water does not
move.

I have come here to be afraid.
I came for love to bundle
what was mine. I am scared
to sneak into the hut to find your coat.

When you put down your pick,
when others wouldn't sprag
the mine's passages; when you said no:

soldiers, who do not strike,
thrust
their bayonets into you.

They were told to.

The young mayor, shitting, closeted
with chain on his neck. I want to

push my hands into your blood
because I caused you to use yours.

I did not die; love, I did not. All the parts
of England fell melting like lead away,
as you showed me the melting once, when you and the
men
with you were jabbed,

and without tenderness, were filled over;
no psalm, leaf-like, shading the eyelid

as the eye beneath is dazed abruptly
in the earth's flare of black light
burning after death.

The spade digging in the sunlight illuminates the face of
my God.

Blind him.

(Untitled)

Concerning strength,
it is unequal. In a paddock
by Stakeford, slag, with bushes dripping
over stone, a horse crops, slowly, his strength
tethered into the ground. The Wansbeck
shivers over the stone, bits of coal, and where
it halts a pool fills, oily
and twitching. Closer to the sea, it drops
under a bridge, coming to ground
where the mind opens, and gives uselessly to
the sun such created heat, the air
cleaves to the flesh,
the bench facing the water, sat on by old men.
If this goes, nothing; this clearness
which draws a supple smell through old skin
making a pause for it. Houses and scrap will heap,
and flake, as
if organs of the soil clagged
with shreddings of rust.

Platelayer

(for J. M.)

'I did not serve, but was skilled
for fifty years, laying plates
measured as carefully apart
as seedlings.' The line came
west from Morpeth, crossing
the third road for Scotland.
At Knowesgate, four houses
group on a bank, set away.
A station was built there.
'I laid plates for eight miles,
but short of Morpeth, sledging chucks
that held the rails; kept them so,
although this has gone now.
Yet here are four pines of
the five I put in. And here
I helped to concrete that
that was the goods bay.
My dog has sixteen years.
We both suffer the heat.
And yet her owners had said
that she must be put down.
I did not say that. And the lupins
strike through the platform;
with a better chance I think
they'd have not done well.
But what I think is that
my work was finished up: five years
past the track taken apart.

No, not so; now we've cranes
to hoist the lengths that we
laid down, form on form. Also gone
a certain friend, who finished
when I was made free.
I shan't work any job
twice. And this is strange,
having the letter from the man,
although it was not him.
Yet surely as like him
as the bolts drove in.
"I can't think of your name
or what you are. You must
excuse me and I have
nothing to tell you and
why I am shut up here
I can't speak of with nothing
to speak about."
But still I am certain
the track we built was skilled,
although you can't tell that.'

The People

(The people are: Finn, his wife Kye, their son Adam; and their friend, Stein.)

I Growing

Finn

A dog howls over stubble fields, where smoke
wavers between two straight trees;
no sounds billow frost-marked hedgerows.
Yet he uses distance, his bark dispersing
as smoke in the lull after harvest before spring,
that taints, by London, the country air.
I turn off to where my wife will labour soon,
gravid in blood, spinal nerve. And quit
heavy winter sharpness, with sullen empty light
reddening grass-tips, hair on fruits' skins.
What is at home? No sound mixes the door's
jarring its hinge. A voice. Yes, I answer.
Each thing here is childbirth. Metal bowls
cambered like shallowed buttocks, the hefted slope
of another is her stretched belly, in the weighed
drop to her cunt, that opens. She calls.
The pouting track's soft firmness dilates;
jugs gleam, wide-lipped, prepared for dropping
water to grin in lolloping mirth; the stable, working pan
will get the flow bent onto the wheel turning
to wash the pounded ore.
Come up love, Kye asks. The stone and wood room
having winter flowers, a fire banters
its tongues onto their erect blue flare.
One other is here, her friend, large-boned: sit, she says,
in your own house. Laughs. He'll not be long.

How do you know 'he'? we each ask her.
By his size, by that, with his slow turning
about. But there's the kettle, and ring the nurse.
Kiss me, Kye asks. Her brow gathers
moisture in the furrows — ploughman's sweat.
I wipe her and kiss her.
                              Below fire heaves
behind iron, intently heating a pot
and sinks into itself, moulting ash.
Its vitality itches terror into the wood it eats;
flesh deciduates in passion. I love this girl,
who is making our child. The nurse comes;
her stiff apron is white and terrorful.
I am upstairs, Kye asking to hold to me. Warmth
beats across her fear and mine. Her fear
is of what makes in her, mine's a white subtraction.
Yet she holds to me, as I touch that swollenness.
'Now' she quivers, 'he stretches me, love.'
'Now hangs back in me.' Yes, a hump,
and sullen, feeling no joy rooted here. But we
wait for its first shove, as it is
to issue rushing, cord knotted, cut,
and reversed into the navel. 'Now', she breathes. If she
pushes, I can't tell if he does, or it's she.
'Hold me,' she insists, 'no, don't.' Fastens to my wrist. I
                                                    suffer
no hand, but its grip. Sweat shakes off again.
Her bowels move, and open. Then, at the parting
of strange lips,
her child, clustering, heaves a gulf open. She pushes,
now contracts, heaves wider, and it is going to come.
It is. 'No.' A pause, renewed, for its coming.

133

Rushing out. Has it? It does, and the spiral wreck
of abdominal life terminates, the creature stirring it.
Even as he's lifted, slapped lightly
for his first breath, self slips its greasy portals.
I will not see him unnamed.

Kye, for his necessity, from hair to feet
is specked and salt, her glistening
moist as placental amnion.
Now it is, for cleansing, the water's turn. Poured,
capable and clear, into the cool, a milky
fluid dripped precisely, and her body washed. Never
as helplessly lying, of excreta and blood
sponged gently. As grass is plaited in a crown
for the May's queen, sovereign not of herself
but of each one's May; as, blithely, in equal parts
each of us is the May, so she is washed.

He howls. Hunger, she says, here — pick him up. Mid-wife
by each, she lifts him to the breast. His mouth
tenses on the suckling milk. He's fingered to her
in such sticky untangling he will unpick.

The pans are hard at rest; we would be glad for as much.
A dog barks
splintering light. Coldness stands up
and full of care, puts both arms
about the house.

Stein

            At eighteen
my first journey, at length. Though not specially.
The gates, on pain open;
a signal, its painted alpine station. Beyond,
numberless circumscription.

I'd my circumcision, with,
in Riga,
the same shit: a Gentile's. Love, we'll be plucked
like a tooth
rejected in its mouth.

I am a great way off from anything.

A wind reverses each cloud through the boughs
that notch the tip of this adjacent moon.
A step in England's calm feels lyrical.
Then past the house I see her tramp. A wind
tightens her skirt above her knees, tanned lightly,
and creased. She is political, she says,
formed by the party, and then used, who would
be used, taking from her her youth, as if
a ghost despondent of its flesh. It is
the cause, she says. Perplexities that creep
from her allegiance wince, as the mouth speaks,
tamper the vigour prompting its bare skin
that wears as anxious to prove serviceable.
Ruthlessness pauses lightly, knowing it gets
her generosity, scores it away
until the bone probes at its skin.

Stares at a number sweated through my shirt.
Naked, I'd swathe my wrists. The furnace eats
flesh, and sweats dust.

Lying in Buchenwald, the British trucked
in slinging densities of ash, as one
walked through it clothed in brown and lifted me
up in his arms. I felt like a mild plant
and shame cringed me, but he was crying. That one
should be cried for, as if a plant had worth
beyond its fruit and serviceableness;
outside the staked wire heaped a pit, and spaced
an equal area from two further ones.
A mass grave, and the indifferent botany
of herbs branching a pungent sullenness.

Those whom I touched I left, that the mind wept.
Salt's fiery labour, bolting fuselages

with her who ceased.

I should have been born as a word vouched in
a Yiddish lexicon. Love, I cried once;
no person answered it. Now, now, voices.

Finn and Kye

What is it that will not eat mash from a bowl?
that lets the spoon come to its lips, then ails
and weeps, or, if the spoon pries past them,
weeps and chokes? Or being fed,

vomits his mash entire.
Earlier, as if that mesh of him were
my making only, and that he won't eat
my care alone, and I could, alone, unpick
his belly's tightening
she flung him on his back, hard, over the bed.
He lay astonished. Then huge tears swelling
the eyelids, came away from him. Silence
breaking with moisture on his cheeks.
I felt what he might learn. Much anger, bruised
in hatred, he got thrust down with. From me,
his wetness on my stubble, cowed by her
that he could see. Deliberately, she asks,
why is he silent, and, why does his food
not stay with him; what is his quietness?
I can't reply. She smiles: it is as if,
she answers, he's made perfectly. As if.
As though perfectly made, but in him, life
moves very little — love, it is not there.
Then hesitantly, but then, instantly sure
she lifts him,
holding him to her with such tenderness the slight
widths of air between them, as she slowly brings
him to her, yield and tense in supple
passion endured by both. Instantly
he cries to her, long, slow, insistent, rising
to screams, as he tenses his head from her.
She lulls him, his pained flesh swaying her with him.
It is as if, she says, pausing, in him
nothing joins. As if that tissue in us
that forms an Adam has not met in him.

I might tell him; but how might I, blithely
as my lips on his penis, or as with brimmed
a softness on his quick as that
is tight in him? Why won't my sweet intent
not pass from me to him, as I took in
his well-planted, minute, sturdy seed?
Yet how, love -- where in him the tangled sense
of nerve-web in the well-held inner bowl
that sups the discontinuous splashes of shape
and feeling that form memory, which is him?

She tilts her head; a grin, being obdurate,
edges the eye and mouth sharply. Some mirth.

I am, yet what I am no man has touched.
I was made slenderly, you know; fleshed at
the buttocks;
my hair is long, and light, and hangs.
My head draws at the back into a curve
that implicates a mind webbed in a brain.
My fingers are long, and small, and my waist
tucks over its hips. Two men
were there before you, and no other one.
Yes, but this should not flatter you, for here
I exercise my choice. Love, oh my love,
you touch my breasts and they excite. You kiss
my flesh as if you loved me. But my lips
force a smile sometimes I do not half-mean.
I loathe this. My mind is not dainty; tough,
perhaps, and pert pert as a bean, yet, so,
irregular. Love, if we do connect,
we have a child fresh as a white berry --

I speak no more of it; what we have made
is beautiful, I know; and tenderness
will sour in me if your neat courage deserts.
Whatever he will make, he should grow soon
my literate intelligence, with it
your shrewd imagination, sharp as sand
and newly cut, edging the mind's thin blades.
He should have — love, lift him, and see if you
find in him our minds, joined up in that new,
that lithe, unbaulked, hurtling intelligence
so beautiful to see; see, there, I think I felt it.

II   History

Stein

1

A certain tale-bearer
                            treads the horizon
and things converge. History has its limits.

I write down nothing of experience
I was combed through, like the head-louse.

I make up nothing
                        from others' print
nor satisfy
                the need for some key-figure

but in extremity, budded
                              and was pressed
between leaves. I made up
history in the lump.
And what of it I was I can bring
upwards constantly. No wreath of judgments
pricks my forehead.
                        Uncertainly I'll promise
to bring an opinion, after I am dead,
as a mild ghost stirs benevolent for talk
on earth, beside a steaming hearth-fire.

Oh my love, virtue was not dropped
from between God's thumb and finger. Going for it
hoarded like a small cache, being opened, it yielded
droppings, as if who is virtuous.

2

If my people were to forgive the enemies of my people
                                          there would
be no forgiveness for my people. Mother, Mother!

III   Testing

Finn

The office of London's
welfare edges the river. Not hope's
prospect, pilasters
bloom acanthus. Stone

faces rhymed firmly
echo confidence. Stone widths
at the forecourt disdain
the river, below, silvers

tidally with us, —
dirt, the dried skin of London. The way
to enter is through
front doors. We will, with Adam,

for doctors, their tests,
and our relief from hope with unhoping
care. No trees; water
that's to this stone what

we are. Stained
with tea, the fleshless soul, the complete
purities, gone off.
Mother, Mother! these buildings,

us in them, integers
conflated in the common good, the common-wealth
magnified by its hand-servants
to the power of one.

Kye

We have sat four hours, with Adam,
that tests may be made
added into such choice
he can't know we make.

The trailing corridors, lights regularly
spaced between mahogany doors. One is
opening for us.
Adam feels cold, sweating lightly.
The temperature is lowering; the anxious
chronometrication of London's business
in this slight chill, where we live
netted in its jurisdiction.
Adam is sweating, coldly. Almost a year.
In the marble jamb a fossil
unfolds a shape we enter.

Kye

Up on his toes, it is amazing how,
the man creeps from behind our son, and brings
before him a huge bell, clanging it hard.
Adam continues smiling. On the couch,
naked and tranquil, no jolt of his breath
until, a minute after, a thick sigh
dismaying the held silence, shakes out.
Startles us. But not him, nor him. A bell
with no responsiveness to it. A sigh
shaken out from the child's watched silences
elapsing then, definitively shuts
this winter's interview.

What silence, with what effort. The trained finger
barring the lips, his voice quavers through phlegm
blown off the lungs, the ejaculatory
opinion, fined by logic down — the forms

imaging science, and colourless as dew.
The earth breathes out. The business, as is normal,
shut into words that close the test. The tone
is natural, and sparkles decently
with worth; the nifty instruments replaced
unneeded as unused; writing is done
niched in behind a desk, as London's madness like
the waters of the Thames through London's council drifts,
and is checked.
                    We feel,
in glances, relieved, his work certified. But Adam
is proscribed. And we
being young, with no further obligation, entered
upon the state, its ample lap, its breast
moistening him.

It is what I have done. I feel, used by
using these instruments, what this man feels.
Adam with smiles is grasping seriously
the adult finger in his palm. Is love,
using this knowledge, love? let it lie there.

This is the letter, which the hospital
will take him in with. Leave him there. And try,
with that life in you both, to grow whole with
a second child, but not identically,
I mean. He stops. Conceive another life
since that is what you must. Rises, and stares
over the oiled, and sliding wateriness
whose soiled dispersions pour onto Vauxhall.
What may I say? I do not know the words
of comfort for you. Goodbye; his outstretched hand

the nails round, their moons lightly white,
a circular cleanliness. I pick Adam up
weighing as much as I, smiling again.
Give me the letter, I say; Finn gives it.

Finn

Air that pricks earth with life, and turns as it
returns to darken, in the year's midnight,
thins in a chill distraction. Winter sun
burns a low arc through the horizon and
is absent. As we trudge the area where
our child is lying, this soil is trodden by
the mad, who, at the next spring, but that is
at the next world, may, with its flexible sense,
elide by that stark light the vacancies
in their maimed circuits. If no world unfolds
these dead may rise to, if the flower half buds
a flesh that does not know itself, and does
not open in a separate flowering,
and touches signs which touch without a trace
of healing correspondence, in this world
will have to do. She, who drifts with her group
of friends, as if we beckoned, leaves, and is
behind us both. Her shape bends gently down.
Her large quiet hands, her breasts hardly there,
an independent mildness, at the mouth,
branched past the cheekbones, brushes to the eyes
widening in hunger.
She gazes, and lifts my hand up slowly to
her lips; then kissing it, releases me

with care, gently, and leaves. That gentleness
forming, without submission, as she kisses
my hand gravely — who shared in that kiss —
in which instant sane or defective; shame
at my dividing question. Walk a bit
on to the ward. Out of its souring brick,
bird-like, the mad alight, shake, and fold in
their movements to their bodies, gazing queerly,
or quiver in recognition, timid, but pressing
on us to touch us over our hands, or faces,
or touch us with their eyes; while everywhere
their mild untrained gaze forms the unsure part
in creaturely connection. And as I feel
her hand, earlier forms shed their flesh, leaving
this bare. Twelve almost, to test
my sanity, I squatted on the pavement
and put a marble on my tongue, closing
my mouth on it. If I could swallow this
and die, I was insane. Or if I left
it balancing on my tongue, then I was mad
to do this. Our child for them is mad.
We reach the twilit ward. Adam lies in
a bed as if an adult. Through his face
his blood, making the skin chill, dampening it,
stirs. He breathes, yielding a changed breath.
We labour it, and press it, the lungs
that can't be relieved, letting it from them.
She rises, and slowly, as she brings her mouth
to him, her lips widen. Lightly, and light,
as if she were withdrawing, as she sinks
beside his silence breathing, she lifts up
his head, and lightly kisses his eyelids,

his mouth, then, as she puts her finger to
his palm, turning his head to us. The eyes,
eyes that are firm, breath in a changing form
moves through them, with a flickering softness in
its shape. Over and not obscuring that,
the moisture of his body
swelling the eyes, and widening them, brings
the life that concentrates, searching itself,
to grow connections in him. Forming him,
formed, and held like this, it connected us
to him, holding us until
that moisture pressed with a thick
movement from him

IV   The Chair

Kye

                Adam's chair is cut
in lions for arms. An amphora unfolds
a vine that flows up, straight, enticing to it
two massive birds, in whose beak-jaws, of wood,
a leaf of wood is shared, linking the chair's
wide back. Two griffins, standing, weight their fore-legs
over the higher branches. It seems dead
to me; no, it is threatening, and I must
remove it
        but fingers stitch, a pink
        nubile obedience, — silks
        of floral vacancy.

A mimic pause between us, then he lifts
a glass, and, with a little shrug he drops
the thing. This does bore me, he tells me, then,
who does not now hear, causing me to wane
against his ear. I love him yet, and loathe
what in me's teased the vulnerable; but watch
the muscle tighten, with some flickering
under the eye, that signs a violence.
Not that he'll see, I flinch. Then, precious flow
of joy through me at his passivity;
then, shame at this. He says, 'the house seems ours,
yet barely; passage through which loneliness
vacates. Were nothing else here I would want
this chair, four-legged, in a ploughed-up field.'
So much, I think, for images, and am sharp
and hard inside me . . . can't avoid our pain,
he says; can't we, I ask; we can do more.
He says, perhaps. It is our pain, I say,
we cause each other, or do not; I had
the labour, the stretched terminal closenesses to
our child. And that suffices. Nothing in me
created death. We did, he says. Then I
do not remember that. Sit there, he says,
hands clenching it, white as his face behind
the wooden vine, the lifted triangulars
of birds. 'Or is this dead? Sit there, if it
is not.' A pause. 'If it is, watch me then.'
   What may I answer, but must stare to see
him raise it, and the facial muscles which
fasten a little glare, switched through the neck.

He breathes; he lifts, pauses, and swings the chair
against the wall. What then? Twice, I think, twice
and smashes it. I see it splintering,
the flapping birds, dropped through the tearing vine
that rasp its leaves, the fruited clustering vine
and tendrils spread upon them; each of these
winces apart all that imaginable
tenderness we had our marriage-day.
And lie, flinching. I will not see. My face
weeps in my hands; salt is one white, death makes
another in us by our child. I was born
weeping, into this.

Stein

There is no language, some say, that could speak
of this. And some, no language that should speak.
Hush. Pure language, language must be clean
of blood. A fine incontinence of love
may not indulge the sufferers. Then, wheesht.
Language is pure, has autonomy,
a life not to be tainted, and its sense
has pure separation from the thing
referred to. Words choose, and they do not choose
a moral valency for blood. And others
'save me, save me', they stammer, who reject
the blade they would not use. Tendernesses
runnel these folk together milkily;
the bitter herb regales a rawer flesh.
And again, language, they claim, tarnishes
lugging the obscene weight. A great steel

from its self gleaming, keeps its inner life
pure of rusts. Wipe it. Faintly I hear
more of this, but not much. A tiny cough.
The throat flicking its ease; dust from a coat,
a ledger of the saints, flick, it is gone.

See, it darts. Quick, firstlings come. Grasp them
before they vanish. Threads that gossamer
I did not spin. Take firm, gentle hold.
Use us, these forms repeat; as I am, so
shall they be. My past at the junction with
their separating lives, I must use quickly.
Guards coughing; the cold bore down their words; I lived.
I should make that mean something, if for those
whose lives despair. I will try.

Kye

So that, therefore, I must
unpick our marriage. Death likes

not it nor Adam, and,

the garment lays in halves.

Stein

A candle burns its white
deep-seated thread, the wax
of hot soft light that shrinks

into itself. I have saved
a remnant, a terse stub
of light, which glimmered on
the murdered, to deplore
what I have lost. And as
it finishes, I would be
a pool of hardened wax
wanting thread on a plate.

So that there is no point
in telling anything.
I need light to outlast
itself that I may live
from it. But then
the simple gout will flick
its spot of fat into
my sight, and drop in through
its dark. While yet
the flame is on my face
of a shared narrative.

V Camps

Stein (1)

As each of you sits, hear me, please.

Which is, two images. The town clustering
over a stable bluff; of desultory

brown rough clay, and stone. Houses light up
above the river's tidal gleam, unslips
ocean merchantmen in on the sea.
In gear, tugged; blithely salt spirals off
the stable wave-form prow. Prepared enough.
Pointed north-east into the Barents sea.
The second is a park, bedded and clipped.
Laurels unfurl loose bloom. A bench in wood
upturned, its short iron legs uselessly stiff
and pointed upwards. Screwed into its back
'for Aryans only', on a metal strip.
Closed wagons are drawn in line through wind, and stop.
A melted cry behind a sealed door.
Some hush. More then, then, more and more. The train
jerked on its wagons, covering them with
its steamy patch of roar, billowing the park.

It came. The Polish engine, sweating, among cold;
its steam breathed over snow. Wagon doors
pinioned back. Mostly the guards with dogs stood,
as we filed in. Patience, and our murmur, wavering.
Neither the young, nor the elderly, wept. Once, a guard
gently helping up an old man who faltered.
Some vomit, softly, in lumps, falling past the edge
of a truck. Prayers made. None bidding us safe conduct.
In a woman's back
the butt's thud. Her body gathered, and chucked
into a wagon, with the doors pressed to
sealing the cries that pressed their shapes on them.
    A jolt, and the train started
its riding inward through a plain of snows,
black in a straight line, scissoring this blank in two

erasable and equal whitenesses.
Urine and fear; the fixed erasure over rails;
stench ravelled through hunger. Three days, round my
watch.
Food, crammed in our pockets, as we had thought to,
outlasted by shared thirst and hunger. Neither heat nor
chill,
stuck in the darkness fixed to earth that paused
over its sullen axis. Occasionally we halted.
Nothing. One further stop, the double note,
someone said, of a plane, of many, encroaching.
We were bombed. After, the grinding on. I could see
nothing; my hand in hers, or my arms upon her
as if dancing. Sleep, torn at length
by a last halt. Voices in German pulled
and pinned back doors, and she and I stepped through
a huge space, as I dreamed, of emptiness;
with here, a bird, pecking
in snow by the svelte guards; their neat
white alpine station, the signal shut across our route.
The station-master in Austrian railway toque.
I thought that I must laugh. We showed our documents.
Barbed, through the snow the high dark live wire, staked.
My fear, dense in my breath. I smelt ooze crushed
over a man's hair, helmeting him. I
stepped back. He struck me. Stumbling, I thought,
I have nothing to show.

The women were stripped before us on the snow,
whiteness skimming a whiteness, dazing me.
Running, as ordered; such election for
what might be seen, what could be seen I watched.

Some fell, with cold. I stood there, but one man
ran to a young girl. Laughter. A nod; the blow
let blood into the snow. Some girls were jabbed
to run, no breath to cry with, and they dropped
abruptly, caught in that soft uniform,
the prick drawn stiff against the trousered leg.
My mother was not seen, nor she I held
through darkness in the train. We were not notable
enough to sift in the first choosings from
this forced community, of Poles, and Polish Jews
mixed in with those who sold us, but were yet
included with us. I was glad of this.
For as we were defiling to our huts
I thought I saw one man who lived a block
from us, and who, in hate, discovered us
to those cleansing the soft snowed earth of us.

We left, or dropped. One marched, searching the step
none kept. I could not quite touch her, as we,
too marked to try to seem unnoticeable,
were led, flanked by the guards, into our huts.

Some nights inhaled the shortest days. Such air
speckled with carbon. Huts, inlaid with us
in double-layered bunks, continuously re-filled.
We were filed, by district, as though we were a map
sections of which, as the figures melted, emptied
the signs whose grid crammed tightly on more of us.

An image of a ship sails, with two more,
milk at the salt prow, nearing. The sea
blinks; in its eye a tanker stretched off-shore

turns on itself away. I watched three ships
sail in through Christmas, wind, churning the pier,
to flap the sagging cloth. The masts slip bare.
Men with their bags step through the deck, and swing
onto the stone quay, past the figureless crane.
The hawser's taut, clinched at the capstan's iron.

These images remain for good in me.

Stein (2)

At times raw soil grazes my eyelids; I
need death to take my shape, a cleric who
might fasten me to it, or, possibly
the doctor's care. One touched me, once; I winced
in perfect health. One fractured the camp.
Each smiled. The first, with powders and advice
tended us. The other, with a rack
of probes, stared at the flesh never anaesthetised.
Each guard made sure he had a health unflawed,
half-matt red, like rouge over onion skin.
The snowy bank sweats; smiling slits the heap
of shapely whitenesses, unfastening
the flesh. Formed by some blade a fistula
stops up the blood.
The mouth curves to its mirth. Extended wings
shrink, and the feathery flesh flails, and drops. Some
argued his skill. Flesh struggles, but it yields
a virgin figure of endurance.
He found its point, and did not move past it.
In terror the flesh split, with pain; and ceased.

Or was deformed, unskilfully stitched up.
One of them used up half an hour of pain
helped to her bed. The guard, discovering her
rising askew from it, beat her. The first five
lining the huts in coupled layers got beaten
every dawn. The blond intelligenced
vigour of the morning guard, my hair
silken as his. God was struck by this, suffering
imagination's growth. I think I glimpsed
a quizzical, wild thought pursing the mouth.

Once I saw how a guard, while shouting at
a boy, pulled from his tunic a black half
of bread, passed him it, mouthing 'juden juden,
arbeit macht frei.' No one is sure. Some thought
God levered on an elbow painfully off
the floor. And those who on the noon's dot
walked to the chambers and did not walk back
said that the quick of Germany went still
and, listening, heard its cry. But I did not.

I stayed my mind over a heap of pistols.

What seemed the point was keeping the whole mind
intact, stopping the flesh from withering.
We were not much to rat or to a thing
that wanted sustenance. I kept two cloths
as handkerchiefs white as I could, white as
is said a whale-bone is. Crushed flat and squared.
They were the whitest square inside the camp.

But wasn't there, Kye asks, one person there
loved by another. In all this, she said.

The word is scrupulous, and has a hinge
with fear, fatigue, or boredom moving it.
True though. A man, holding together metals, stood
by a woman who bolted them, observed by a guard.
Sometimes in their work they touched. The guard
flinched as he saw this, sometimes hawked, and moved
away, or he would bash one of them. Both
endured the blow; each was of the same town
married in Catholic Poland, black-haired deicides.
In the camp there seemed not a second pair
more careful of each other, or, of a stranger, than
these two, aware, at any instant that an unfelt
chipping of care, some little blunting
of sensitivities eroded them.

They were a silent gathering-point for me.
A paired calculus of intent human
scrupulousness linked in our mutual drabness,
by which I, and others, I felt, could measure up
our actions, so, humiliate the self
by suffering selfless inequalities.
These two bore a seal of privilege, given gladly
despite the thread of equal fairness and unequal
needs common to us.
                        Once the guard found
her working alone; a dram lacking counter-weight.
No rape; he offered her for her husband white
fresh bread; she took the bread and gave it him.
The white, the fresh, his mouth filled with no words.
But just that portion lifted in him his flesh
a gloss above hers, noticeable to her.
She smiled; some muscle pricked over by a nerve

tensed her. She waited. And the guard approached
with more bread, pricing it. She took the bread
and not its price. He struck her, hard, over the mouth.
She, cupping it to her, dropped. No one was there
watching. This, also, her husband ate. She feels
the cells that multiplied on hope use up
and not replace, as on her arms he touches
the greying down.
Her upper lip grew thin, to him fragile as bone.
It came. A fixed proportion of us to stand
and line the chambers, while the rose pricks through
its pins of zyklon. He and she both heard.
As she, her flesh then weakening, shaped her choice
and, as it shaped, chose her life, shading hers
from his. She lay still in her bunk. Although
as he smiled, rising up, she gathered all
she could into a smile, softening the face
yet with as much as what they each had felt.
An ancient smile travailed her face for days,
hovered like gas upon the mouth and eyes.

That little life, Finn said, as if it could
have saved itself. You do not know, Kye said.
But he is listening. Dust at the eye,
upon it, smears its soft expanding shape.

A second pair worked underground, and bolted
metal sheets, sleeping in the hut by ours,
as equally crammed and as consistently
sifted by gas. These two met in the camp.
No joy in her. She had coiled her hair, tying it
into a huge, fair, glistening knot, piled heavily.

Her left hand had no middle finger there.
She'd brought to wear a broad belt; buckled brass
hooped up a woollen, grey, stained dress. Round him
as he absorbed her gaze, the air went tight
and fastened him to her.
She had a child by him and it was dead.

No quickness, and no moisture; but a thick
vitality. She was alive, she loved him.
All of her face was thin, and like a cry.
She had a brother here, who hated him.

He had been picked out as gauleiter in
our group, choosing the Jews, a Jew amongst
more Jews; a scholar in authority
with no weight, queer with theologies
wedge-shapedly tapering to a blunted edge.
He pre-arranged the sequence that we filed
the chambers in; some cried their needs, he used
a deft and moistureless logic for the queue.
He was in education, it was said;
able to calculate, an integer
of their device, recurring terminally.
He drew the good meat, queued by some hatch that
we did not line, and, pliant as a limb,
food, pliancy, and reading melted him.

Smoke rises off the stacks; feathery soot
catches the wire. A man walks, hands catching
his thought between them. Guards rose, noiselessly,
strapped to their rifles. Those who had said 'no,
they would not go', were taken up from there.

Some said his ledgering was correct. Gathered
among the next figures was Elsë. Her face
ached with vitality. Yes, death, she said
erasing his name with hers. It kept him there,
wiping his cap across his hands. Passing,
she almost glanced at him; and still she took
the cloth's pattern into her glance. He stood,
no turn changed with hers. Her breath pressed, I say,
through us.

VI   Some Growths

Kye

1

What meaning, asks Finn then, his tone cool
dabbing a brush precisely, its touch light,
what meaning can this have? — a boy's small plea
I once mistook for innocence — Must I
suffer these images, unlike the dead?
They left whose pain died in them. Through no fault
but patience, I bear some of theirs in me.
What were we made for, then? My dead touch me,
open my care, by right. And as I look
past Adam's form, it is mine stares from him
at me. It is sufficient, it is all
the grief I need, as I can gather to
my hands for him.

2

In startled fingers this boy took
pity, the wounded intimacy.

Finn

Love, oh my love,
my gently abandoned roots

nothing in me like those
faces that lean through him.

I would be as much whole.

Stein

She touched Finn's sleeve, but what was it she touched?
The modesty through Finn glances his cheek.
Yes, it is possible. My form touched with
her care increases. Small insistent rising
equilibrium. She turned from me

and tough and lucid, formed
an independent shape.

Fear's oceanic is a ragged moon
opposed by hope. Childlessly, night walks on
long legs, and puts both arms about the house.
Melted, or simmering, we place cups
in our preparation turned
aside for a further thing.

A Shetland Poem

At Grobsness, a house
mild-visaged above the sea
had three floors; the roof
and its wood hold.

No other beams.
A minimum of elegance spared
in stone. Twelve slabbed frames
admit all that comes.

Dung stamped hard
onto the floor, gorges
the blank mouth of the hearth.
The house fills.

A shelter for beasts
the best they may have had;
when we disgorged
from the steel cavalry, our crofts'

flesh thinned to
water and shards. Wasting
grasses spindled some wool
skeined loose.

The wind staggers itself.
With stone broadcast
on low peat slopes
touching water.

Child-absence, absence of women
and the dank flit
of beasts useless save
to the industrious visitor.

But by what we had
before, not worse;
and the slaughtered had not
this good dirt.

Shouldn't we have, by
a tally cut against nights
chilling inside the moon's
crubb* of frost,

wanted, and got, more than
a pinched nissen hut,
fish, skin flayed, the storm's
goring shove.

The ribbed vessel, with sheep
was lifted, and jiggered
clumsily on rock, a creature
stricken beyond repair.

The doe of the sea.
We were not. But what we were
worked under hundreds
of moons icily lugged,

*crubb circular stone wall within which cabbage seedlings are
protected.

we were slow asking for.

We got from each laird
the fish's head, the crimson liver;
now we have the whole lot.
But less the dead

the depopulating
war, the multiplying thickness
of the Atlantic magnitudes.
Of the sun, a flake.

A pale ameliorating
glüd† quickening
the coil, in us it stiffens
and presses up in mirth.

The throat lusts for its oils.
Joy, joy — spills, and makes free.
We are going to drain, drain and crush
the spent beer-can.

Civilization eats out
the blood from the heart;
the laboured gratitudes
between us and earth

make a lace-tented shawl such
as women excruciated from
threads marled round bitterness.

†*glüd* the glow from the lights of a town seen at night through mist.
Note The two glossed words are from the Shetland language which
is in effect Icelandic.

A Second Shetland Poem

If you had to choose, I asked her, which of

them would you have? One tongue, at least,
dickered upon the palate, the words,
like fish in a creel, packed on each other.

In the late summer, its small startling beauty
touching her hair, she answered. Their meanings
skeined together, her words were clear:

I would have both worlds.
But choice forced on me,
I would have the best of each.

Through air sloping past the voe, each still
thing seen, a car rode, and, altering its gait,
reclenched on a slow third; its exhaust
smutched the air, the fine machinery
breathing perfectly.

With a smile she turned from this. Walking up
the low slope, she re-entered her house, and took
to herself her solitary form.

In the summer wind, with no haste in it, the smile
dissolved, and the wind reflated earlier
contours of itself, its tress blowing
out over three miles of water.

Isaiah's Thread

1

Cry. What shall I cry: flesh is grass.

The billow stiffens; the wheats are no longer supple.

Whom are we to send? One we relish
as fresh image of us; he can petition
the little widower.

Then I said, here am I; send me.

The almighty Father, Prince of the grazed fields.

But I saw the fly, its life webbed.
And crouched on its alphabet a voice, crying,
shall the axe boast against who hews with it.

Go go go, it said. I flew into the earth's rim.

And grew cautious. No indeed, I answered.

2

The lion sniffs the moor's hair; straw-specked wind
upbraids saplings into the trout-mouthed voe.
Out, it said.

What shall I cry? Cry. Why must people by people
be torn?

Yes, I said.

I undid my hand, and fastening to it
a stone dilapidating from a house, crouched
in the grass's time.*

I was astonished. Shall they abuse
the creature melting through the field.

I waited with open eyes. Men automatic
with rifles defiled singly across
the fragrant and depopulating croft.

It is a question, I said, of love, and gripped the stone.

The fly will be appointed, the sweated ox;
and a furred leopard, over the kids it has pastured.

Lie together, grin, creep, pant, assemble;
convene the kingdom.

* *the grass's time* — Jon Glover's phrase.

from

The Little Time-keeper

Gifts against Time

— Ella Pybus

1

On the insufferable flesh
over the creeping haulms, light

gauzes with saffron; and the limping soma
yields its psyche. The petite desert woman
crouches;
death's parched foetus.

Vulnerable hand-maiden, stay.

2

Who stays? In abundance
torches of sable light, in pustules soot
on the dump of after-life.

The livid melancholy of fat.
Extinguish
the greasy flambeaux, death stays.

3

Spiritual contusions:

serpent of roots, whose stung shape
writhes upon the earth lashing
with the prowess of miracles.

Be Moses: throw light on the wriggling bronze
over rock divine with water;
get memory quick with pictures
for our aching forms. I take

responsibility for
the fleshy images
I bring with me past death.

Tolstoy's Brother plants a green Stick in their Estate at Yasnaya Polyana. It has happened before.

Sydney 1974

The woods at Yasnaya Polyana.

Eyeless leaves
rustle their neighbours' faces. Sough.
Sough: the wind. Tolstoy's brother
plants his green stick.

'If ever you find
this carved secret, Earth
will have greened a Paradise.'

Green, green.

Blackmen, abiding their wilderness,
scorch the defoliated, wriggling grub.

Whitely the ferry chunters us
between bays. In oiled dispersions
of wateriness we sprinkle to our rest.

The cut religious stick fades
among first plantations. Wind heaves.
Wordlessly, it vanished, bearing
what the hand gave, of brief warmth.

171

O supple Paradise. Integument
prime as our mother's breasts
folding milk.

The pouched marsupial intelligence,
its care, its teeth, stained with grass,
its leap to the peaceable kingdom, that,
that and no other thing, where is it?

The greening of a cut, wordless
Australasian stick. Wind lifts
like a huge leaf. Lovely questions
foliate the Pacific.

South Africa's Bird of Paradise Flower

Sydney 1974

In flower it is an idea of self
as bird; two nacreous tapering ears.
Nothing tappers in them. No hammer and no drum.

The neck flexes. Its cerise bird's-head
gouts its juice. It colours cerise.

Its ears plume. The head is a lower jaw;
the upper beak, a spindle with blue flanges.
Why no matching? Five rivets stud
and pair this creature to its under-half.

It unfolds deception. Two plumes listen,
and a silent beak emits lucent gum.
In Africa the black skin is black.

Not two plumes now, but swells, and pricks
a further pair, a second violet beak:
two birds rejoice over one neck,

and the body replicates huge leaves.

So fine the mode of words is its ghost.

The flower is its first idea. Rammed with
so much of itself, it furthers other selves

that multiply. And will not take flight,
rooted in austere bright irruption.

The Excellence of an Animal

A sombre cat outstares
mild food, and that absorbs
the tentative black cat.

Your cry – its calculating
delicate balance of abandon

connects: your jaw fangs
with milk white hairs.

All your excellence has left you.
That is not true. Footprints

tacky with life pursue
their owners. Winter noon

strikes through its brilliance.
You are a black leaf

the pavement steps over.
Maythorned or grimed the car's

grim elegance consumes
the road, with a barely

apprenticed transfiguration
of lust two people quench

in the gear's change. The straight
road hits you; his woman's

moist basis transfigures
the breast's fleshy compassion.

We prised open your mouth, and there,
a little drench of blood
between the tongue and the palate.

Cat. Cat. The small head
eats our sight, as winged fleas

quit their host: as sin drips
from our dead.

All creatures with their ghosts

in any form, bring
yourself free of the wheels

The Plum-tree

Our grave spittle covers his face.
Afraid I insult my God
of my poems I'll say little.

We married in late winter.
Mild as a pear, whose succulence
lured its priest. Yes, I said,
I believe; and miracles
balanced on pumiced hands. My door
glided shut.

I speak of the six million
and do not shave; no iso-rhythmic
evennesses of mind temper
the blithe compliant ratchets of industry;
and for the earth I work off, I earn
how much? We consider, and feed
the excellence of three cats.
When the sun undoes its pure,
fierce hands, I talk with the plum-tree
in the dene where mild limestone
kneels to the ice-floe. The tree's
incipience of fruit makes plump
the maidenly flowers: to what is torn,
wrenched, shot, or beaten, it can bring
nothing.
The dene's light crumbles. Of no use
if beauty affirm the techniques
work anneals; and, what droops away

is beauty as consolation — in the flame
work is of cash drudged for.
Barren are the plum-tree's flowers
fleshed as they glisten.

One image of continuing trouble

A prayer cup

As if steel, but a silvery
tar creeps upon Isaac
in Abraham's hand. Our Bible

is clasped in darkness. And for wine
three inches of the blood
of six million. The cup

wells Hebrew, and my grandparents
have tracked their kind into
the lake over-flowing

our curious feet. I who write
a factious poem want the means
to bless a christian. Breath

from the two locomotives *Work*
and *Freedom* steams over
the numbered faces.

Arbeit macht frei ('Work makes freedom') mottoed the camp gates.

Untitled Poem

The perfume on your body, and the musk of it.
The second is on me, I smell the first
on you as a sign.

I wear the undelicate odour.

Shuffling through the city, my mildness deceit. Hungry
and light-headed with venom. The adder silks
to refuse bins.

Fastened to the street: the working men's hostel past
two bins. A man beat me to those. I was afraid,
and the pulps he left stayed unfingered.

I had not thought of you: timidly
I spent my pence. In a dormitory
my body covered my trousers.

Along your flesh drifts your hair, a tree bearing
concupiscence, and your smile shows.
This is enough almost.

Your arms are slim, your fingers' amazing strength.
The tree's whole self blurts through long hair.
It's not grief, not joy; saffron spills
milk on the road.

A friend working through television gave
me a brass thruppence;
I bought tea with it, bearing nausea.

In Jerusalem the hills, bare; soft-haired goats
made of teeth; all the shoots are champed.
Hunger drifts through plains, over the declivities
of London; delicate smoky flakes of it.

On the rock splinters cold air; a coward
felt another's bruises in his groin.
He fears the cold air, its true match. Love, I love you.
Can I mean more?

You smile among four friends; three of us speak
and you say nothing. It hurts; your speech
is a silent woman.

Each night the kicked man screams.
If I help you. If I can lift you. His stain
over stone is blue, feather light.

The feet of police emboss the sidewalk.
                            Linked
by my penis, our child could grow.
                            Fear
synchronises with us.

I enter you. Local as a root. I wait
for you to get your breath. We measure each other.

We are prepared, lassitude melts. The hair
is naked, the piled spaces of hunger, and I touch
our candour;

the flesh in abandon robes gently
the tenderness. The candle's flame curves
round its inner light.

Your hair is sea-weed. You smile monstrously.
Memory flushes me through.
Your salt skin rustles on me. Of love, this entirely
is not what we were taught.

Thin black coffee in a pan flicks
beads of heat. The flaking city mounds
stillness, and amiable sleep
spreads our flesh.

We will not last, love, as we are. Love,
I would have us stay, ever, like this.

My conscience, my fear, and our sex, stir.

We want to Survive

Sundown. The candelabra branches
seven flames. Sabbath is a taper.

The half-world douses sundown's fiery
indignant moral forms. Although

(surely) earth at its poles, flattened
like an orange, where blenched winds

precipitate with no end — earth tires;
inside that night we are its fires.

Is it against fire that one prays
each seventh day? Is every prayer

subliminal with earthly fear?
It's dark and the candles spit lightly.

Like hotel functionaries we hiss
with insulted life, who shrink with fire.

The cantor vomits wax, grease flares
his eminence. Six days worldly fat

burn on the seventh's consuming thread;
is fire the meaning prayers endure?

Admit the mind through fire. Of no sex,
on the burnished silver flame assigns

as equal mild deliberate fire.
Look, Isaac; and do not touch.

Self makes its fire. Each outer flame
selves its next flame that bears a fire

gravid with inmost flame, no flame
that does not burn, is an unburning

inner moist wax light. I bring

my grandparents in an image in
inside the inmost flame. Old men,

someone's grandparents, though the sons
and their sons' sons are ash, someone,

some old man holding to the slack
rough skin of an old woman prodded

past child-bearing, some old men
are still grandparents. And they putter

their Hebrew as the cuffed wrist bares
and passes moist bread, that the hand

has blessed and split. Take it, Isaac,
since you know the language. The moth consumes,

and Hebrew prints the wings that sheet
in fire. An unburned darkish moist

prefiguring resumes the life
of memory that neither loves

nor does not, linked in dissolution
to what dissolves, but does not go.

Not just yet, Isaac; no, not yet.

From 'The Little Time-keeper'

Entropy at Hartburn

Between the hoof's cleft loam squeezes;
so beasts enter night-fall. Steamy
presences; the dunged breaths falter.

Hartburn divides night on itself
with a shutter. 'Mildred clamp out the dark.' Cream lace
embroiders its holes.

The huge energies untwine, and stars
slither away on the braids. The wagging stems
of sex slather to inane fruitfulness.

Not a thing to comfort us. The holly's fruit
taps at the church's stained glass
where solstice clenches its day,

and small energies out-thorn, the profusion
of winter at mid-night.

At Nightfall

Night-fall unfastens the door, and the font
baptises the raw body; womb
and its flesh pule to each other.

The mother's milk: clear and sweet
dropping from the soft pointed opening.

It's the stars count, and they flee us
inundating their absences
with our terse lives. When we die
we are dead for ever.

It comes clear finally. The Milky Way
vents its glowing hugenesses over
what's not there. The galaxies
pour their milk away.

Nothing's going to last

the clear baptismal water, twice welcome,
like two good hands

like the olive with
its stone of oil.

Shadowing

Upon one straight leg each steps up-hill and burgeons
through a year's ring;
their leafs breathe.

'Clothes.' No, not clothes.

Arboreal men, shadowed
by leaves, so

shadowing us
we sliced our flesh from their shades

that cut away, the trees lie
acquainted with the shadows of death:
for which there are words
and no language.

Give me your branches: the woodsman
handles their deaths: a blade and its haft.

Then us. Earth washes away. Leaf,
leaf leaf

like treeless birds

Shades

Cheviot: makes silence of
life's bare soft maximum,

fluxing not much. No, hangs

its milky fluid in
Henhole's vacancy; plump

bellies of cinquefoil mixed
with the Barren Strawberry ooze

their lobed flesh at the cleft
Cheviot turns into;

and through the soft
crushed odours, what trees?

The Elderberry and
red-berried Ash, not here,

in the North's summer dense
with shades. Do they

grow in us; do our selves form
on theirs? The Oak's

rooted head branches joy
with leaves close as wood-grain

with between them birds
numerous as mustard grain.

Not here. And yet here, even
so, the passions of form.

I need you. Who else,
who else but you?

the huge strong soft presence
with roots; robust

musical presence

your shape
of noise ghostly

with permanence:
                    Tree.

Centre of Absence

Names for one street: Pandon?
The same course
winds hesitantly to decay.

Pampedon is *Pantheon*. The Roman site
opens a Greek name: *pantes theoi*
all the gods. Oh, yes;

the city will scrape this
from itself. Mender of graves and teeth.

Clop: the worthy feet counsel
speculative contracted powers.

Stars burn in the simple dark;
our dense lives fly.

First, Jew-gate: rain sluices silver
braiding usury on the stones

with workmanship. Newcastle buys
the Jews' expulsion. The King

is all gold; Judas bit small
in the coin's realm. So, the King's light

clatters upon the streets. 1656,
'Come in again,' Cromwell stutters.

Jew-gate, in traceries
of despair

the systemic fountains
of prayer and flesh

Trade's filigree rubbed
of instinct; the steep street

slithers through vetch and ground-ivy.

Over by the Quayside, as if a hanged man
cut to morsels, size of a dog's mouth,

nothing. Decayed commerce

transacts melancholic Scandinavia
in desultory amber beads. 'Ye divvent

knaa nowt heor.'

Breaking Us

1

Moss sprinkles its cry; in the bowed
fields of wheat, poppies
flutter themselves.

Love, come on.

We hand-cut stone fruit
in the lintel over the door.

Blessedness in that.

2

Turning its arms, the caterpillar flails bricks.

This section is almost ended.

Tears that would come
press back their springing.

A cry flutters on mudded tar, its road
a wheel that unrolls, hastening.

Street sellers of innocent fruit
are touched by the police.

The lintel with fruits, splits.

3

Smells of tea on the shut
curtains. Winter's light
puts its arms round the house.

Touch me, she says.

The rug at the fire, and the fire
warm us.

Love, our child conceives
amongst wool and the milled
white bread touching you.

4

So much spills. The look
you gave the house
goes down with it.

The wheel drives downhill, mudded
in under the Tyne. An oiled rag
stretches to brine.

Our house, love, done in.

Wind dusts dust with it.
Their plan unfolds in a flat way
a flat road, where the rug
laid our thighs.

There, dust off clay blows from
the despairing chimney breasts.
Nichts, love.

5

What we have been given.

Given? Brick for chalking on;

the rush through the eye
of the summerless high-rise,
each jot of dust rented.

Dust off the armaments
smokes into our heavens. Consecrate this
constructed at the rim
of the city's eye.

The cheerful councillor's face
gleams off the earth.

'All power to the constituent city assembly'

No tree, grass. The caress
of it at best the going
drab daily.

Love, we are dust, owing rent.

The rag stretches to the sea.

This section is also done with.

First to Last

1

The Milky Way: a chart, a conducting
of white bodies
lit by time in darkness. Off

in another place, spirals of milk
curd that darkness. If we fell
to where would we fall? Prodigal forms

that pour away.

There's no grasping them: no name
reveals the parent

in heavenly nakedness.

2

Here sprouts Meldon: *Moel-Dun*,
a hill
shimmered by cross, by cross or sign:

to house, to haven; in 1242

the needful light.

Church as a long room, chancel and nave
one plain intrication. Snug house

a round low vault of stars
ceilings in blue crosses, blood and blue,
shadowed with gold.

Were we gentle, so would this be.

3
Traumas of smoky shadow.

Bolam: of two names one
forced on the other: swollen ground.

Creation names her groin.

But before this, where we cut
their shades from us, place of the tree-trunks.

The likely pastures char.

Sheared from Rome, the Causeway
runs off. Poind and his stony dog
mark the foot's emigrations

grass persists in. Mound and stone

ponder the North's shadows:
the acreage of green farmers
under huge leaves annihilating
in shade their greenest powers.

Amongst the tumulus the short
dolerite coffin, grained with soot
upon the lumpy

glutinous flesh. I can't say.

For what's there, what is it? eyelid
bereft of coin, no bones
tumbling through earth. The grave

envelops no name. Death
has burnt away.

And smoke, lingering.

What can we Mean?

who didst stretch forth Thine arms upon the cross, to draw all
men to Thyself . . . give peace to all nations
The Flodden Prayer

1

The prompt field of battle

is a chart, on which
men deform each other

a well, course-pipe pulsing
its lush onto the soil.

2

A proud Prince, through England . . . a King
etched over Scotland: the drums throb
upon the furled heart's beating
in equal brotherhood of pain.

Blood paints blood; is this
to be human, above mouse, or the oiled
fur-clung otter? Flodden

notches the ranks, and the rank
is a gap in the tumbling line.

Cry, what shall I cry? Our flesh
is grass, a withering
its clause in the syntaxes.

Soil recovers its right mind
however heaped is ditch
of blood or burial;

the living are a wound one
upon the other. Sunk flesh
and the tried soul perish. 'Flodden'

the mind bursting its soft
root of blood

3

He harries another. There breed
no wounds to the battle, none,
but the shared nuptials of death;

slowly haling the body
from itself, that bespeaks
its mutilations. Stop that.

Sopping the green worsted, blood
pulses on, whose bare pain
death shags many ways. Enough;

but pleasure's innerness, silence,
voices lust's fury, his body's
very breath. What does

it matter what we do
to our lives; the stars

will freeze their milks apart
in equilibrium.

The soul nourishes in blood.

4

It is the discipline
of strong men that clasp
the weak into strength's ring.

Clap your red hands, our pikes
devour their flesh; jawbone
brays in an ass's shape.

Were it in us to be
as God, and break his covenant,
we'd rive soul
to the spongy equivalence
of torn life. O, then,
by all means, purge and disperse
each nucleus as if
a blooded soul. Donor of light.

Life through our pikes, we cast
our arms wide.

The Church is getting Short of Breath

Sabbath of the pensive spread buttocks.

Conscience, the size of a dried pea,
chafes over the pews flesh sweating

its Sabbath juice.

Douser of burning wax: old man
hugs remorse like a first wife. What labour
will such bridal pains be fruitful with?

First night of marriage wakes the bride
to shimmering kindness; our hemisphere
dishes the Sabbath, dead prayers,

the dulled rose of texts, desert mica.
Air breeds to the shy nibbling tourist.
Work-day fingers the rosary of work-days.

Work's necessary bead, — the mechanic
wrenches the thread by which our lives
fasten to us.

Coming first to church, sharp
as the warrior wren. Morning dews
the prompt mind, tourist of the holy
places pious with no use.

This is the true debating-ground,
and here the praying hands consume
the life they build. I shall do what I can.

The question loses its memory,
and the dense shade, in the spaces, runs
to hydrogen

laconic as its dull copulars.

Sneck the latch-door; Adam from sculpted
wood raises Eve with himself
to the bridal shapes. Love congregating

the bench will have its forked play
of their clasped forms: I have come to an end

of the ancient days. Laboured tweed
surplices the rich man.

My lovely parents, when you shaded
each in the other's thought, and flesh
pleaded one anatomy, of life,

endless life, death's frail nucleus
sweated to come alive, its soul
in our flesh. I loved my origins.

But you mid-wifed death. So I became
man, and as others judged me you
I judged. O gentle God, with both hands

you lathed prayer, a chariot's flange, God
of hope. The stars' system contracts,
that, or they flee us. Of such fountains

we lie in the solar ground, and the question
loses its mark.

Index of first lines

Index compiled by David and Linda Wise.